RAHU AND KETU: OUR KARMIC DESTINY REVEALED THROUGH ECLIPSES

Joni Patry

Publishing Services, cover, text design and editing:

Published in Dallas, Texas, by Galactic Center
http://www.Galacticcenter.org/
4442 Manning Lane
Dallas, TX 75220
Printed in the United States of America
First Edition

DEDICATION

I want to thank all my students and particularly my beloved tutors and friends, Joelle Foster, Shreekla Ram and Rose Reveley who have inspired my work. I could not have built the University of Vedic Astrology without them.

My husband Daniel has always been an inspiration, giving encouragement throughout our lives together since we met in high school.

I have three sons who have helped me throughout my career as an astrologer. Christian my oldest son helped me understand the financial world, while my middle son Preston helped emotionally. And as this book was being written my youngest son has had a profound effect on my work. Therefore, I want to dedicate this book to Austin, who has helped me in so many ways.

Called the voice of reason by his peers, his wisdom outshines his years. His calm and patient demeanor reflects his sweet soul and spirit. He helps me with every aspect of my life and business. As an entrepreneur, he knows social media. He created my YouTube channel, helped edit the videos for the University, inspired and filmed my Facebook Live videos, and built the educational programming of the University of Vedic Astrology. Everything that I do has been enhanced by his assistance. I look forward to seeing Austin's own successes as he ventures out into the world as an entrepreneur.

I have an incredible 5th house for children (Mercury, Neptune, Sun and Saturn in Libra). And whereas the 9th house represents the 3rd child, the ruler of the 9th house is exalted Saturn in the 5th house. I have great gratitude and love for my dear sons. Our love and respect for each other will endure through many lifetimes.

TABLE OF CONTENTS

INTRODUCTION

Rahu and Ketu are forces that reveal the deeper aspects of our soul through understanding eclipse cycles. They give us information needed to understand how to heal our lives through all aspects of our world via relationships, career, finances, health, and our spiritual growth.

Rahu and Ketu are the hidden aspects in a chart that reveal unknown issues concerning our life. Rahu and Ketu have an 18.6-year cycle as they transit through all 12 signs. To better understand the unconscious issues surfacing during an eclipse cycle, it is important to look back to when Rahu and Ketu last transited the same points in your birth chart. Likely, it means that 18 or 19 years ago you experienced an issue you will uncover again now.

You will come to understand the use of eclipses in light of your personal attitude toward your own private struggles – the psychological aspects of your mind and the illusions that control your behavior.

This book is structured to provide an understanding of Rahu and Ketu in the natal birth chart. Their placement in the zodiacal signs gives expression to the personality, and illustrates the meaning of human behavior. The houses they occupy reveal areas of life that our karma dictates we are meant to experience – to facilitate the soul's highest growth due to past experiences in previous lifetimes. There is a table provided with the sign placements of Rahu and Ketu from 1940-2040.

Rahu is the entrance into this illusory world of Maya, and Ketu is our exit to a spiritual world that while in the physical world offers imaginary powers. Therefore, Rahu indicates our future and what we are here to discover in this lifetime. Ketu represents our gifts from the past, and can determine what we brought with us in terms of good and bad karma. Together they direct our life in the here and now, as future prospects unite with the legacy of the past to create our destiny in life.

Eclipses are the most powerful tool for prediction we have as astrologers. As Rahu and Ketu transit through the signs and nakshatras, joining with other planets and stars, many forecasts are based on an understanding of their past cycles and results. This gives the power to make predictions for the future.

There are many yogas or astrological formations with these shadowy planets that can indicate destiny, as evidenced in the charts of the rich and famous. An analysis of presidents, billionaires, musicians and the famous highlight the results of these nodal combinations. They give an essence of destiny, eg, in the Kala Sarpa Yoga when the nodes contain all planets on one side of the chart, or when the nodes are conjunct certain planets. These examples will give you a deeper understanding of what these profound and obscure shadowy planets can produce. Once you understand the roles of Rahu, Ketu and the eclipses, life will have new meaning illuminating core issues through the horoscope. All the calculations in this book use the Sidereal zodiac used in Vedic astrology

CHAPTER 1

Rahu and Ketu: Our Destiny

Rahu and Ketu are indicators of our destiny revealing our past and future. The houses they occupy in the chart indicate the areas of life that will be relevant throughout a lifetime, especially in terms of the greatest lessons they offer. The signs they occupy flavor the experience but, most significantly, the planets that rule the signs of both Rahu and Ketu give the essence of the soul's karma. Rahu is our future, indicating what we came to do and achieve in this lifetime. Ketu is our past, including the karmas we carry from pervious lifetimes. Together they give us our present experience, the blending of the past and future. This is the now.

Rahu and Ketu open the door to the soul. Who are you, where did you come from, and where are you going?

Rahu and Ketu are called the shadow planets. Astronomically, this is because of the shadow cast by the Moon upon the Earth during a solar eclipse, or by the shadow of the Earth upon the Moon during a lunar eclipse. But the notion of shadows also suggests they are indicators of our shadow side. During eclipses, it may be that our shadow selves are revealed, or something that was hidden from us surfaces. This can be painful but, inevitably, it's always healing if you take advantage of these opportunities.

9

Every 18 months at the time of the eclipses we need to assess and analyze what's being revealed to us about our shadows, and look deep within to heal. This can give us some of our most powerful lessons of life, and serve to heal the karmas of our soul. Rahu and Ketu change signs every 18 months, therefore the eclipses will successively occupy different signs and houses in our chart. The house and sign will indicate the lesson and message relevant to our life's current experiences.

A planet in your natal chart within three (3) degrees of the solar eclipse will embody a message with a radical shift and change to come in the following year. Eclipses are life-changing and are sometimes referred to as a wipe-out, meaning a new beginning through a profound change, like a message board erased to clear the way for something new. Eclipses through the agency of Rahu and Ketu can also indicate fear, due to an element of the unknown, like stepping into the void, that emptiness before the entrance into a new world. In a way, it's a kind of death, like passing from one world to another. We're afraid and can't imagine what we don't know. This is one of the manifestations that eclipses can evoke when contacting a natal planet.

There are two specific times each year when a solar eclipse will occur. This is when the new moon is conjunct Rahu or Ketu. There is a new moon every month but there are only two new moons a year that fall within the designated orb (18 degrees) with Rahu and Ketu in order to effect an eclipse. One new moon will be with Rahu, the other with Ketu. They occur exactly six months apart. Rahu and Ketu are also called the lunar nodes. They travel backwards in the zodiac and from one year to the next year they move about 10 degrees backwards.

Rahu and Ketu change signs every 18 months, thus altering the effects according to the sign they are in for both world awareness and individual perception. As we'll see in a later chapter, both sign and house placement of the nodes are significant.

The signs that Rahu and Ketu occupy, and the relationships they form with the other planets, contribute an influence on the collective unconscious and, consequently, world affairs.

The signs Rahu and Ketu are in for 18 months at a time are the signs in which the eclipses occur. Therefore, if Rahu or Ketu are conjunct other planets at the time of an eclipse they will stimulate world events relative to what that planet represents. Planets conjunct an eclipse are engulfed in darkness and the shadow side of that planet is revealed. This brings to light something to be healed. For example, when the eclipses conjunct Jupiter it has an effect on the economy since Jupiter signifies wealth.

Planets conjunct Rahu and Ketu at the time of eclipses will see their effects magnified. The aspect to Jupiter and Saturn affect financial and social affairs. Similarly, the aspects of Rahu and Ketu upon the outer planets, Uranus, Neptune and Pluto are transpersonal provoking world changes, consistent with their nature. Mars is always a trigger for events and is conditioned by the sign it occupies when aspecting the nodes. The inferior planets (Mercury and Venus), with the nodes, also exert an influence at the time of an eclipse.

CHAPTER 2

The Sun and Moon: Astronomically and Symbolically

The world of duality implies an existence in which we may be confronted by opposites, sometimes even extreme polarities. Planet Earth is our vantage point, a world in which these opposites are made manifest. Yet here we must find the way to balance these extremes.

At least some aspect of this duality is reflected in the astronomical makeup of the Sun and Moon. They may be considered as fundamental to your existence because life on Earth is so profoundly influenced by both. In astrology they're considered the "lights." Aside from their actual luminosity, they also have the capacity to illuminate both our outer and inner beings. As such, they are prime reflectors of ourselves in this world.

At the heart of our solar system, the Sun is the giver of life. It emits the warmth and light that makes life possible. Because of this, the Sun has been worshiped in many cultures as the Supreme Being, the primal force of nature. Without the Sun, we could not exist.

As Earth revolves around the Sun, this annual cycle creates our seasons. Because the Earth is tilted somewhat compared to our orbital plane, our northern and southern hemispheres get longer or shorter days during different phases of each revolution, thus influencing the seasons. This orbit, which takes 365.25 days, measures the span of our terrestrial year. Meanwhile, the Earth's rotational period of 24 hours creates each day, when the Sun dawns anew.

These are the yardsticks of time via which we measure our existence. During daylight hours we're active and conscious. We exist in the reality of our world. During the night, we sleep, and sometimes witness the activity of our unconscious mind through our dreams.

Throughout our lives on Earth we scarcely stop to think we're living on a sphere hurtling through space. We feel like we're standing still on a flat surface. Our perception is not the complete reality.

In fact, our perception of the world is partly an illusion. We experience our lives through the medium of our senses, which are synthesized and given meaning through the agency of our minds. The world is one thing, our minds but a partial reflection of our terrestrial reality. From this vantage point, we could say nothing is real except for what our minds tell us.

From our perspective on Earth, the Sun appears to revolve around us. This is a geocentric point of view, ie, one wherein Earth sits at the center of our *perceived* universe. Similarly, we view all the other planets in our solar system as revolving around us. From our perspective on Earth, this our perceived reality.

All of our experiences are set up as an interplay of dualities, which are based on polar opposites. Astronomically and scientifically, this relates to the positive and negative forces of the magnetic poles. We have a positive and negative charge that creates a balance that keeps everything in constant motion. This constant motion is relative to vibration involving the atoms and the planetary spheres.

Another level of polarity concerns the experience of night and day, which is caused by Earth's rotation. Within this cycle appears the Moon, which revolves around the earth. This is a powerful representation of dualities – Earth's revolution around the Sun, as well as the Moon's revolution around Earth – a cycle within a cycle. The Moon's orbit around Earth creates the pull of the ocean tides and changes in our atmosphere.

The Moon actually spins on its axis too but since it is locked into its orbit by Earth's gravitational pull, its spin is completely synchronized with Earth, so the same side of the Moon always faces us. The dark side of the Moon symbolizes the unconscious side of our nature of which we are unaware.

The Sun and Moon reflect the duality of life on Earth. The Sun is the active, masculine, positive force (polarity), providing the light of day. The Moon is the receptive, female, negative force (polarity), which shines only in the darkness of the night, indicating a time of reflection and rest. The entire earthly realm is based upon the concepts of male/female, father/mother, giving/receiving, and day/night polarities. There can't be one without the other. The parallel in Chinese philosophy are the concepts of Yin and Yang, two forces in constant flux and balance, where yin is passive and negative force, while yang is active and positive.

The key to life is finding harmony between these two forces on earth. The perfect balance of these energies exists within nature, and lies within the complete organization of the geomagnetic pull that regulates the perfect spinning of the planets on their axis.

There is perfection of the cosmos and how it manifests as duality on earth. The Moon reflects the female; a woman's menstrual cycle corresponds to the Moon's cycle of 27-30 days. It takes 27.5 days for the Moon to circle the zodiac, and 29.5 days from one New Moon to the next. The cycles of Sun and Moon reflect the cycles within our bodies. Understanding the planetary cycles of our solar system gives us a better understanding of human cycles within our world.

The visible bodies of our solar system — Sun, Moon, Mercury, Venus, Mars, Jupiter and Saturn — are related to our chakras, the energy centers in our bodies, which are in turn connected to our glandular functions. The base or root chakra is related to Saturn, the reproductive or creative chakra to Jupiter. The solar plexus is related to Mars, heart chakra to Venus, and communications chakra to Mercury. The head chakra is related to the Sun, and the crown chakra to the Moon. Energetically, through the chakras, it's as if we have our own solar system within us, thus creating a link to each of the planets.

The Sun provides light by day, while the Moon reflects sunlight during the night. Nighttime is when we sleep and recharge or bodies. At day's end, we withdraw from activity, go within ourselves and lose consciousness of the outer physical world. In sleep we embrace our inner world, the domain of our unconscious mind. This unconscious mind reflects upon and assimilates our experiences of the day. But when we awaken the next day, we're effectively reborn, a mini-cycle in the much larger process of life and death. And each day this cycle repeats itself — born to a new day, living our conscious worldly experiences, then succumbing each night (like a death) to the unconscious realm. This reflects the process of life and death for all beings. In a way, we never die, but only exchange consciousness for the dream state, enjoy a rest and gather our energies again for a rebirth.

Every cycle on earth has the same process of birth, growth, culmination, death and return. The waxing and waning cycles of the Moon reflect this process. The new moon is the beginning, a new birth, and it continues to grow in light until it comes to maturity as the full moon, the culmination point, after which it becomes a waning moon, receding in light. At the end of its cycle each month, the waning moon disappears and then begins the entire process again. This is symbolic of the process of life's beginning, ending and renewal − a cycle that never ceases.

In viewing the Sun and Moon as symbolic of our actual life experience, we tend to forget an important variable that affects this process of cycles, which is that it is only seen from where we're standing. But when we're in the eye of the hurricane, we can't see what's going on around us, and therefore can't understand the process. Earth is the central element of this cyclic process involving the Sun and the Moon, because this is where our point of view originates. The number three builds upon duality to complete our world. Spiritual texts, for instance, represent this trinity as God the father, the son and the holy spirit. The father is the Sun, the son is Earth, and the Holy Spirit is the Moon. The Sun is the giver of life, the Earth is our experience, and the Moon reflects our inner spirit.

CHAPTER 3

Eclipses

The relationship of the Sun, Moon and Earth brings us to the physical manifestation of the eclipses. Within the process of eclipses there are shadows involving these three spheres. The most fascinating fact is that when aligned each has the same apparent diameter when in a total solar or lunar eclipse. During a solar eclipse, the Moon perfectly obscures the Sun. During a lunar eclipse, Earth's shadow perfectly obscures the Moon. How is this possible when they are all so vastly different in size? This is no coincidence, and is symbolic of our existence as human beings. The physical phenomena represent a deep message revealed through the cycles. Astrology is the interpretation of these patterns, cycles and their symbolic representations on Earth.

Eclipses represent a period of inner reflection, because within the darkness of these shadows, what is hidden can reveal the secrets to uncover the truth of our lives. When the unknown becomes known we may experience an epiphany. This is possible within ourselves, because the mystery of the universe lies within our own psyches.

Eclipses occur during a new or full moon. A solar eclipse occurs at a new moon, when the earth aligns with the Sun and Moon. The Moon is between the Earth and Sun. It is the Moon that crosses in front of the Sun and blocks out its light. During the day the light of the Sun is obliterated from sky. In ancient times this created panic and fear because people believed it was the end of the world.

At the time of a lunar eclipse the light of the Moon is blocked by the alignment of Earth between the Sun and the Moon. Earth's shadow covers the Moon. Lunar eclipses occur at the time of a full moon, either two weeks before or after the solar eclipse.

The Moon's nodes map the points in the zodiac where the Moon crosses the ecliptic, the apparent plane in which Earth revolves around the Sun. At the time of eclipses, the Moon is also aligned in the same plane, allowing it to obscure the Sun, or Earth's shadow to obscure the Moon.

The points where the Moon crosses the ecliptic are constantly moving. This movement is always relative to the motion of the Sun and Moon as seen from Earth. These points in space are symbolic of Earth's interaction within our limited cosmos, the solar system. This is all about our earthly experiences, the duality of the Sun and Moon engaging with the third element, Earth.

The Moon's orbit around Earth intersects the ecliptic at two points. These two points are the called the nodes of the Moon. The north node of the Moon (Rahu) is the ascending node where the Moon crosses from the southern to the northern hemisphere. This symbolizes birth, an entrance into material manifestation. The south node (Ketu) is the descending node where the Moon crosses from the northern to the southern hemisphere, symbolically an exit from the material world and into the spiritual realm. So Rahu takes us into the physical world and Ketu takes us out of it.

The Sun and Moon symbolize the father and mother who give birth to this world. They are integral to the symbolism of our experience here on Earth.

In the Hindu myth of Rahu and Ketu, a serpent slithered between the Sun and Moon to partake of the nectar of immortality that was being given to the gods, who are symbolized by the planets and luminaries. When the thief was discovered, Lord Vishnu threw a disk, splitting him in half, but he'd already swallowed the nectar. This division severed the serpent's head (Rahu) from the serpent's tail (Ketu). The fact that it had come between the Sun and Moon alludes to the fact that this point causes eclipses. Rahu and Ketu are referred to as shadow planets. The shadows cast imply a universal truth – that which can't be seen or understood constitutes a mystery of life. Our conscious awareness is blocked as we enter this worldly dimension. We're cast into darkness and emerge as life on Earth, influenced ever after by the Sun and Moon, whose symbolism is woven into our unconsciousness.

As we're born into this world the awareness of the other realms from which we've come are forgotten, blanked out of our minds. We're suddenly separated from our past, and now beginning the process of learning through the thinking mind.

Rahu represents the head consumed with the thinking mind. But mind separated from spirit creates illusions, and Rahu is the indicator of worldly illusions. Ketu is the quality of knowing without thinking. It is the spiritual connection that can give insights that lead to enlightenment. Rahu is the materialistic physical world and Ketu is the spiritual world that is beyond this earthly domain. But we still carry Ketu's essence within us, and that's what connects us to the eternal world beyond.

All this represents the cycles of birth and death into and out of this world. Rahu and Ketu are the indicators of destiny and fate, symbolizing our entrapment in this physical plane. These shadow planets control us by our desires. Our desires are our karmas. Our destiny is to release the chains this world has cast upon us. It is like the serpent's bite. The poisonous venom intoxicates us with the desire for worldly experience. Rahu takes us under its spell with the illusions of this world, the promise of happiness: "If I could only have more of the things that give me pleasure." But of course, this only leads to insatiable desires. We can never have enough. And since nothing of this world is lasting, desire will always cause us suffering. This is the venomous bite of Rahu.

Conversely, Ketu strips us of the objects of our desires, revealing that nothing in this world gives us security and permanence. It is essentially the process of enlightenment, when we come to realize that, ultimately, it's all an illusion. Nothing of this material world lasts; it's all Maya, a delusion. Ketu is the bringer of enlightenment through the realization of this truth. Ketu is the release of this world. Just as Rahu is our entrapment, Ketu is our final liberation from the karmas of the soul. Whereas Rahu will give things for a price, Ketu will take things away but leave enlightenment in its place.

Human beings spend most of their time in their minds. Although we exist in this world, we're often not part of it because we separate ourselves in our minds. Our eternal nature is Unity and, when not a part of this earthly experience (within the entrapment of Rahu and Ketu), we are one with everything. This is a hard concept to imagine on Earth because all we know are endings, beginnings and separations from each other. That sense of separation comes from the mind. As the head of the serpent, Rahu represents the mind. Our most natural state is to be one with all. To be separate is unnatural. When we're one with all, we feel complete and whole without fear. This is our natural state when in spirit. Rahu can represent fear because it essentially blocks out reality and keeps us trapped in the illusion of this world, separating us from truth or the Divine source that connects us with everything. The knowledge and truth of who we are beyond this world of separation is contained in the meaning of Ketu. Ketu gives us glimpses beyond this world but we can't really conceive of it due to the limitations of our mind, which is a part of the illusion.

An understanding of Rahu and Ketu can lend insight into the meaning of eclipses. Eclipses offer us glimpses of what lies beyond this world. When eclipses occur there's an opportunity to see the truth during the brief unveiling of the illusion. When the illusion is swept aside during an eclipse, these are times that allow a vision beyond this world. This means, that which controls our earthly experience of the world (Sun/Moon) is blocked and we can see beyond it. Even the pattern of day and night is obliterated, because a solar eclipse can introduce the darkness of night in the middle of the day.

In ancient times people didn't understand what was happening and believed it was the end of the world. For a few minutes at least, it certainly would have felt like that. This radical disruption of a normal day would inevitably have provoked some sort of psychological "time out." Hence, to this day, there's still a sort of primal fear that persists around the times of solar eclipses.

A solar eclipse is when the Sun's light is blocked by the Moon, throwing Earth into a brief period of darkness during the day. Symbolically, we might say that, what has been awakened in the dark will be revealed. Even the casual observer will often notice there are more tragedies and upsets around the time of a solar eclipse. I hear sirens more often during the two-week period between the solar and the lunar eclipse.

Solar eclipses occur at the time of the New Moon, meaning something new is being presented out of the darkness, something will be revealed. Two weeks later, that which has been revealed will come to light when the Moon is full. Lunar eclipses occur when Earth's shadow blocks the sunlight that would normally reflect off the Moon. In our emotional darkness the truth may seem obscured, but our shadows will be revealed. Most of us can't bear to see the dark side of our nature, so denial usually sets in. The shadow aspect of our nature prevents us from realizing our spiritual truth.

The solar eclipse is the point of focus, since there may be a lunar eclipse two weeks before or after the solar eclipse or there may not even be a lunar eclipse. Eclipses are determined by the new moon (solar eclipse) or full moon (lunar eclipse) in close proximity to the nodes (Rahu and Ketu). The lunar eclipse is an offshoot of the solar eclipse.

In Jungian psychology the "shadow" refers to the unconscious aspect of our personality which constitutes the ego. It is our dark side that is hidden in our subconscious mind. It is our instinctual nature that we are taught to suppress as children, in the process of being taught morals. Understanding the shadow side can alleviate unconscious behaviors of projection in ourselves and others.

In essence, eclipses bring us the opportunity to see whatever in our being is preventing us from the most important thing we're here to realize — to grow spiritually and transcend the illusion of this world. This process will reveal all of our weaknesses and fears. Fear is a manifestation of this world (Rahu) because while in this world we're entrapped in its illusions. Ultimately, we must come to the realization that this world is only a false perception of reality.

Based only on our immediate perceptions, the sky is blue, while the earth is flat and motionless. Meanwhile, reality is, the sky looks blue only because of light refracted through the atmosphere, and our spherical Earth is spinning on its axis while hurtling through space.

The mind sometimes gets in the way, distancing us from true knowledge, creating a sense of isolation and fear. When we leave this world we'll arrive in a place of unity and oneness with all, where the spirit of God embraces everything. At that point we'll experience a sense of wholeness, completely absent of fear, where all is known, and we realize God is all around us, and in us.

How can we better understand the role that eclipses play in our personal lives to unveil the illusions of the world? This is revealed through the zodiacal position of the eclipses each year.

CHAPTER 4

Rahu is our Future,
Ketu is our Past

Rahu represents what we're here to learn about life in order to grow. These points (Rahu and Ketu) can help us understand earthly existence and perhaps awaken us to a higher truth. Many fear such understanding because it means detaching from what we value in our worldly existence. We fear losing all that we're aware of. But the realization of an all-encompassing truth can reveal what's really important. With this realization comes true bliss and complete understanding which eradicates fear and ignorance. This means no more suffering. This is what the polarity of Rahu and Ketu represents in our awakening consciousness. We awaken to an awareness of everything, which means no boundaries, beyond space and time.

To understand this concept, recall what was important to you as a child or teenager. When you reflect on those childish things you wanted and felt you'd die if you didn't get, you realize how insignificant they are now. But even now, the things you consider important will be just as insignificant in the big scheme of things once you become more enlightened. Remember, time and space and our physical realities are all dependent on our individual and collective perceptions. How are we to awaken from that illusion and end suffering? Most of us can't do that because we're still like children clinging to our attachments. Most of don't want to let go. Our attachments make us feel good. But once we experience loss and suffering, we'll want to grow beyond this world. That's when we get on the road to enlightenment. If ignorance implies living in the dark, to be enlightened means stepping into the light, and thus banishing ignorance.

Ketu represents the inner perception of our connection to the Divine. Ketu strips us of our attachments. In the process, we suffer and grieve our losses. Yet in this time of despair we touch upon what saves us – our knowing that this world is temporal, an illusion. Once we get a glimpse of light beyond the darkness, we may transcend our shallow-mindedness. If we have the desire to grow in awareness, we may begin to see the truth. This truth is something beyond our comprehension as earthly beings, but nevertheless gives us a sense of timelessness, boundlessness, freedom and bliss. Eventually, we'll all achieve this and, if we acknowledge that there are no time limits or spatial boundaries, we're already at one with the essence of God. At this moment, we're only awakening to this reality. Once we pass to the other side, our awakening will be complete, and we'll realize our existence is only an illusion, just as it always was. The power to perceive this truth – that the world is only an illusion – comes under the domain of Ketu.

So now we're regarding Rahu and Ketu from a whole different perspective – that Rahu cloaks us in worldly attachments, while Ketu strips them away. Rahu gives us desires and earthly pleasures, success and riches. Ketu takes away those comforts but encourages us to dive deeper in search of the truth that lies beyond this world. Rahu eventually brings suffering, since everything worldly is only illusory and temporary, and we will lose it as surely as a snake sheds it skin. But Ketu, which encourages us to understand the temporality of all things, helps us pierce the veil of illusion and realize the ultimate joy of enlightenment.

The placements of Rahu and Ketu at the time of your birth will help reveal the way in which your awakening may be realized.

Rahu pertains to our future aspirations in materialistic terms, while Ketu relates to what we've brought forth from our previous lifetimes. Our talents are a function of our past development. These may come easily but, at the same time, may not be of much interest, since we've already achieved success in these areas. Rahu indicates what we might accomplish that is new and challenging.

Since Rahu and Ketu take 18 months to traverse a sign, there are many people born in the same 1.5-year period who have similar destinies and experiences. Although this can affect many different groups of individuals, people born in the same year have a connection and may share a similar temperament.

It takes 18.6 years for Rahu and Ketu to transit all 12 signs, so every 18-19 years, people go through tremendous changes in their lives. For instance, many people graduate from high school around the age of 18, leave home and go to college. Other turning points, whether in mid-life or senior years, arise when Rahu and Ketu return to their natal positions, otherwise known as the nodal return. These occur at ages 18.5, 37, 55.5, 74, 92.5. Often, at these transition points of growth and development, we're reminded of the purpose and meaning of our life.

Within the same nodal cycle, nine years after the nodal return there's a nodal inversion where transiting Rahu conjuncts natal Ketu, and transiting Ketu conjuncts natal Rahu. This creates something of a crossroads period, accompanied by confusion and uncertainty about life's direction, and may trigger changes that could send life off in a new direction. Care must be taken during this pivotal time in life.

Interestingly, in order to enable an eclipse, there must be at most 18 degrees between the New Moon and the Rahu/Ketu axis. The greater the orb between New Moon and the nodes, the lunation will produce only a partial (annular) eclipse. The closer the nodes are to the New Moon, the more likely it could be a total solar eclipse. Coincidentally, in Vedic astrology the dasha cycle of Rahu is also 18 years, just one more case of synchronicity and meaning surrounding the number 18.

CHAPTER 5

Rahu and Ketu in the Signs

To better understand what Rahu and Ketu may mean for us in our lives, the first step is to see what signs they occupy. The sign placement in our own individual charts will have specific meanings. They will indicate important issues and lessons we must learn in accordance with where our past lifetimes have led us through Ketu, and where Rahu will take us in this lifetime. The transiting nodes through the signs will also reveal important events throughout history. These can in turn be analyzed and extrapolated to predict future world events.

Rahu and Ketu are always exactly opposite. Rahu is the ascending node, while Ketu is the descending node. You'll notice they are always in opposing signs, in the exact degree and minute opposite each other. Here are the oppositions of Rahu and Ketu:

• Rahu and Ketu in Aries/Libra
• Rahu and Ketu in Taurus/Scorpio
• Rahu and Ketu in Gemini/Sagittarius
• Rahu and Ketu in Cancer/Capricorn
• Rahu and Ketu in Leo/Aquarius
• Rahu and Ketu in Virgo/Pisces

Rahu is our future and Ketu is our past. The polarity and opposite meanings of the signs are potent indicators, both of our current life and how our past life influenced the necessary lessons that had to be learned this time around.

According to their sign placement in your own chart, Rahu and Ketu have particular lessons to teach us. The typical experiences are described below, both as they pertain to the past, and what we can do now to make a better future.

Rahu in Aries, Ketu in Libra

This lifetime you are to develop your own skills and be independent. You need to stand on your own without any reliance on others. You are a self-starter and a pioneer, going into ventures and the unknown to realize your own potential. In your last life you were all about taking care of others, and were dependent on making others feel supported and secure.

You would become so involved that you would lose your own individuality and identity through relationships. In this life you are to take back your Self to become whole and complete, without the need for a dependent relationship. You can master relationships this time around without being co-dependent.

Rahu in Libra, Ketu in Aries

You are here to develop yourself through your relationships. It is important that you come to understand yourself through others. How others make you feel is an indication of your own character. You will not feel whole or complete without the interaction of love and commitment in a lasting relationship.

In previous lifetimes, relationships always bogged you down, never allowing you to achieve your own personal dreams. You empowered others to achieve their dreams, so now it is your turn. You are empowered by others and have the drive to achieve your desires. You gave of yourself before and now you are the one to stand in the light of your own personal development and success.

Rahu in Taurus, Ketu in Scorpio

Parashara, one of the great seers of Vedic astrology, believed Rahu to be exalted in Taurus, and Ketu in Scorpio. This is a good placement for manifesting desires in the physical plane. Material things are important and are easy to come by.

There is a sweet and gentle temperament that has a love of beauty and nature. A love of life and the gifts of the material world give a sense of happiness and contentment in the world.

Financial security gives a sense of achievement and the ability to provide for the family without hardship, stress and worry. You are gifted with the comforts of this world due to strong desires to achieve and seek power from previous lifetimes. Your struggles from previous lifetimes bring you comforts in this lifetime. You were forced to share your wealth before but now your earnings are yours to keep.

Rahu in Scorpio, Ketu in Taurus

These placements are believed by Parashara to be the debilitation signs of Rahu and Ketu. Rahu in Scorpio can have intense desires and a thirst for material wealth so, if not achieved, will indicate extreme unhappiness. This intense desire generally creates what you quest after. Rahu in Scorpio can give an insatiable need for power. You may be jealous of those who have what you want.

You are passionate and intense and will quest for material fortunes since you're used to these gifts and comforts from previous lives and feel the need to always have more than others.

You are emotionally intense but have a problem with expressing exactly your feelings. Feelings of lack and insecurity keep you stuck in an emotional vacuum that you can never feel complete in the area of love. You don't know how to differentiate love from material things and money, therefore, never coming to terms with true love or superficial love. You tend to buy your love and, consequently, others only like you for what you have instead of who you are.

Rahu in Gemini, Ketu in Sagittarius

In this life you are to develop your mental skills in terms of learning and communicating. Conveying information to others is an art that you are to discover. An open mind connects you to other cultures and different perspectives on the world.

Language is a talent you command. Your way of communicating is so appealing that many seek you out for sales and teaching. You can convince anyone to buy anything.

In previous lives you were the philosopher and high-minded teacher. But now you are to connect with others on a personal level, teaching others how to live on a daily level. You love travel and adventure, but now you are to teach in your community and to the masses who need the introduction to life's lessons. You were the teacher of teachers but now you must appeal to the masses who need your understanding and learning the most. In previous lifetimes you were a "know-it-all," but now you need to develop non-judgment.

Rahu in Sagittarius, Ketu in Gemini

In this life you are taking your intellect to a higher level. Now you are the teacher or guru to others. Now that you're the authority, just make sure you don't overestimate your wisdom. To be a true teacher, you must be humble.

You are consumed with truth at all costs. Make sure you don't become the preacher talking down to others. You must make sure you don't offend others with your high-minded, righteous opinion. Don't push your rules on others.

In this lifetime you are to set the example of love and compassion, not judgment and rigid rules. You must travel the world to teach your message, but remember righteousness will alienate others instead of leading them to truth. Learn to see others' predicaments through their eyes and not from the judgmental perspective concerning your unbending beliefs. Through life's experiences you will become understanding, aware and compassionate.

Rahu in Cancer, Ketu in Capricorn

Cancer is the sign of family and security. It pertains to your need to feel supported and safe. In this life you are to develop a secure and safe place to raise a family. Family values and togetherness are important because in previous lifetimes you were the provider and didn't spend as much time in the home. You worked to get away from the home and never had the connection to a nurturing mother or secure family.

There is a healing within the family unit that needs to be completed in this life. There may have been problems early on in your family of origin but you have to heal the family unit by becoming the cohesive agent in your own family.

In past lives you never felt that you achieved enough from your work, but you were actually an overachiever. Your quest was to climb the ladder at all costs, and never gave the appropriate love and attention to your family.

In this life you are to surrender to the needs and feelings of others. This will give a feeling of purpose and wholeness as old karmic bonds are healed and transformed.

Rahu in Capricorn, Ketu in Cancer

You are to provide and care for the family to achieve greatness in your work. You were the provider on an emotional level in the past life, but now the place for you is outside the home. In past lives your family was wracked by instability and insecurity, but now you're compelled to give your family the financial security it previously lacked. You're driven by ambition because you're determined to never feel the deep sense of lack you felt before in previous lifetimes. Just don't make the mistake of not balancing your work ethic against the time you need to spend with the family.

You'll be very successful financially because you're driven by the past sense of lack. Determination is your asset to have security, with a good home and family. You have the power to achieve financial security to protect your family. In your past life you were lacking the emotional commitment and security that you'll never do without in this life.

Rahu in Leo, Ketu in Aquarius

You are a leader and have a thirst for achievement. In your pursuit to take charge and tell others about yourself, you may forget to share. As others surround you, remember to ask, and listen to their needs and desires. You may feel the world revolves around you but it takes others to make the world go around. As you learn how to value others, you become the most sought after leader and friend, for no one has more loyalty and commitment.

In previous lifetimes you were all about the needs of others who never reciprocated, so you become more and more self-consumed with the self in this life. Learning compassion and unconditional love opens your heart and brings a life of happiness. The warmth you emit outward will draw in many supporters.

Rahu in Aquarius, Ketu in Leo

Rahu is at home in the sign of Aquarius for this is the air sign of the thinking mind and intelligence. Rahu needs to express its cognitive value. Only at times you may get caught up in your head too much, and there is a need to come from the heart.

In past lives you were all about being in control and being in command. Now you are intellectualizing about many things, especially about human behavior. It feels better to share your thoughts rather than to keep to yourself as you did in previous lives. You gave of the heart in the last life and you were hurt and your loyalties betrayed and so now you feel better staying wrapped up in your head to better protect your heart.

You are very intellectual and incredibly smart but you can be arrogant when you're with others not as brilliant as yourself. Be open to others' thoughts, because you're not the ultimate authority of all knowledge. Compassion for humanity is real when it truly comes from the heart.

Rahu in Virgo, Ketu in Pisces

Your attention to details can at times detract from your ability to see the big picture. In previous lifetimes you had the tendency to blame others and be a victim, where the world was a bad place causing your problems. But if you're committed to doing the work, you now have the ability to solve your problems. You allowed others to take advantage of you in previous lifetimes but now you're on guard to prevent others from stealing your soul.

Being overly critical and scrutinizing will deter a meaningful relationship. To overcome your fear of being taken advantage of by others, try giving without fear in order to form lasting sincere relationships. Practice love with boundaries and you'll overcome past relationship issues.

The power to organize and be disciplined is something you constantly needed in previous lives. The understanding heart you had in previous lives will develop the happy love life you're seeking now.

Rahu in Pisces, Ketu in Virgo

Your tendency in previous lives to have constantly worried and created problems has made for a much more compassionate and loving soul in this life. The hyper-critical behavior of before is now a thing of the past. You can let your feelings be known when you wear your heart on your sleeve.

Your lack of boundaries can open you up to aggressors who have little consideration for your feelings. Knowing this, you have to take responsibility for your own feelings and not blame others for the way you feel. You are to look within yourself in this life to understand the effect you may have on others. In the past your criticism destroyed your relationships. In this life you are to be open-hearted and accepting of others' shortcomings. This is a huge hurdle to overcome now. If you succeed, this will prevent you from being the victim you were before.

CHAPTER 6

Rahu and Ketu through the 12 Houses

Rahu and Ketu through the 12 houses give a deeper sense of life's lessons. There is a certain fate and destiny attached to Rahu and Ketu, and depending on what houses they occupy, this indicates fated events. For example, Rahu in the 1st house will direct your life as though you have no ability to plan things because, as you make plans, circumstances beyond your control take you in another unimagined direction when you least expect it. For Rahu in the 7th house, you meet your partner in an unexpected and "fated" way.

Rahu and Ketu have some very specific meanings that may be relative to their placements in the houses. Here are their meanings:

Rahu rules the desire that bring us into this life. It can rule addictions, for it gives but with a price. It rules extremes of life — opportunities and problems, consequences and attachments to the materialistic world. It rules obsessions and compulsions. The house Rahu occupies is where we constantly strive to improve, and suggests our eternal quest in this life. It can reflect our achievements and accomplishments but can turn to addictions and obsessions.

Ketu is the karaka for the outcast in society, and is the spiritual side of life ruling over other-worldliness. It is the indicator of loss, including death. Whereas Rahu brings us into this world through desire, Ketu takes us out of this world. The house that Ketu occupies indicates where there's a sense of something missing, a feeling of emptiness. Trying to fill that void may become an obsession, with the house Ketu occupies becoming a vacuum and a central focus in life.

Following are the indications of Rahu and Ketu in the houses which correspond to different areas of life, plus the destiny they influence through past and future karmas.

Rahu in the 1st house

Rahu in the 1st house gives a sense of importance, since it's a powerful placement for a life of intensity. This gives a life of fate and destiny. As you plan for the future, it seems events sweep you off into another direction that becomes the correct course even though different from the original plan. The world is an adventure of the unknown, uncharted and unplanned territory of experience. Things just seem to happen out of the blue.

Physically, you can be robust and sometimes large, literally and figuratively. Circumstances involving the materialistic world consume peace of mind, and cause many upsets throughout life. Attachments to a world of money and superficiality can destroy your world. But with Ketu in the 7th house, your partners take up a vast amount of energy and time. Steer clear of the victim-types in relationships. They can drain your energy and time. Many times the partner has bright or very light-colored eyes.

Ketu in the 1st house

Ketu in the 1st gives a very elusive quality, the feeling of being very hard to understand or know. There is one foot in reality and one foot out, connected to a vast spiritual world.

You feel unconnected and unsupported, as if you don't fit in anywhere. You may consider yourself an outcast from society. There is a sense of disconnection and alienation, wanting to escape to another world or place.

Many times the body can be very thin and frail, especially in the younger years. At a very young age there may be sickness which is a way of unconsciously wanting to escape the world.

Rahu will be in the 7th indicating a partner who is very materialistic and bigger than life, causing great concern and problems in marriage. It may indicate a partner with addictions.

Rahu in the 2nd house

Chaos in early childhood can create all sorts of emotional problems throughout life. The parents may be divorced or separated. There will be many ups and downs financially, for wealth or lack thereof is an issue from many lifetimes to be healed. Great amounts of money are gained, yet with extreme spending and loss. There's an obsession with money.

Food and drink or anything ingested can be a major problem, turning into eating disorders, or addictions like alcoholism, drugs, or smoking. There is an oral fixation. Speech is important, but foul language and yelling can get you in trouble. Watch out for the misuse of the voice, such as ridicule and criticism of others.

There can be problems with eyesight or the teeth, so take proper care of them. Social problems arise from disrespect, so try to be aware of what you say.

Ketu in the 2nd house

Losses in childhood seem to influence your life. Problems in the family, such as parent's ill health and financial problems, plague early childhood. The stress endured early on creates a great deal of insecurity later in life. No matter how much money is acquired there will always be a sense of lack and insecurity. Financial problems are a source of major concern throughout life.

There are issues around food and drink in early life that influences the life later. There can be food sensitivities, allergies or aversions. Dental care is important since the teeth may be weak. Problems with the throat are due to the sense of never being heard. You felt what you had to say was unimportant and negated.

The eyes are weak and can be sensitive and very light in color. Speech is delayed but can be a great gift later. You may be good at learning a foreign language.

Rahu in the 3rd house

Natural ability with computers is a means of interaction and skill. You can teach others technology, with an ability to understand the electronic world. Understanding of technology gives the ability to make a great living. Work is around unusual people or foreigners.

There can be very complicated relationships with siblings, with a split at some point in life. Siblings may be half-sisters or brothers. You may be an only child or the youngest one in the family.

Early life was difficult in terms of education, making it hard to form new friends because of changing schools many times while growing up. Difficulty hearing, or problems with the ears, is a typical childhood issue.

Ketu in the 3rd house

Losses around siblings create a void in early life. There may be a sibling who dies or has some kind of emotional or physical problem. As an only child you might yearn for siblings throughout life. Early education and learning may have been extremely difficult but a specific talent is developed and gives life meaning.

This placement indicates a different way of learning, such as overcoming dyslexia, but can also indicate creativity and the capacity to think outside the box.

A strong desire to travel the world might make it seem like you never find what you're looking for, but finally realize the answers are inside instead of outside.

Rahu in the 4th house

Intense problems involving domestic life and the mother may drive you out of the house at an early age. Usually the mother's personality clashes with your will. Emotional separation with the mother may be felt throughout life, with an emotional healing that never occurs despite constant effort.

Security is a means to an end, and you'll spend your life dong everything to achieve security. Money, love and popularity will be abundant but the sense of security is still scarce. You may seek the security of a big expensive home.

Ketu in the 4th house

There is always a sense of loss around the home, family and mother. You are constantly seeking a sense of security through home and family but never feel complete in this area. You feel like the black sheep of the family, wondering if you were secretly adopted.

There seems to be a deep aching and yearning in your heart for a happy home life, and the mother you never had. You cannot settle down and feel secure where you're living. You'd love to settle and put down roots but an unnerving feeling that you must move on keeps creeping up and you move again and again, feeling a bit like a gypsy.

Rahu in the 5th house

Rahu in the 5th house give deep mental powers and an ability to control many aspects and people in life. You can be a powerful advisor through your deep intelligence. Many seek your advice. Coming into this life you're blessed with unusual talents from previous lifetimes.

You may acquire wealth and fortune, but experience trouble in having or raising children.

A compulsive and obsessive mind keeps you in a constant state of anxiety and mental worries.

Ketu in the 5th house

Ketu in the 5th house gives a deep connection to the Divine, and an intensely spiritual view of the world. There is a profound understanding and compassion for others. The mind is plagued by obsessive ideas and will have the tendency to be consumed with conspiracy and paranoid ideas.

Be cautious with investments, because your judgment regarding stocks and gambling cannot be trusted.

Children may be a major concern and worry. Overprotective tactics can be overwhelming, for there is an innate fear of harm coming to your children. There is a sense that you can never do enough for them.

There may be loss around children. This may come via divorce, ill health or accident.

Rahu in the 6th house

A strong immune system brings robust physical stamina. Matters around health and healing direct the life in an unusual way. There will be interest in healing health issues, whether physical, mental, emotional or spiritual.

Ambition and drive in your workplace will give you a boost in your chosen employment, but problems around coworkers and staff cause conflict. Working with foreigners may bring success.

Children become strong and wealthy after a turbulent childhood.

Ketu in the 6th house

There is an interest in unusual healing modalities, such as yoga, ayurveda, herbs or acupuncture. The desire to help those in need can lead to your participation in humanitarian group efforts.

You may experience difficult health problems that are hard to diagnose. Looking at health from a spiritual perspective might make more sense. Love of small animals will bring many pets into the home.

Employees and coworkers are undependable and irresponsible. There are many problems for children at an early age.

Rahu in the 7th house

The partner is powerful and overbearing in many ways. They may have an addictive personality, so be careful around this issue. Their fun side could turn dark and destructive if not kept under control. Extreme events will plague the marriage, while suspicious tendencies of ulterior motives may cause problems. The partner is very successful but obsessive in their work, spending very little time home.

The maternal grandmother has a colorful past, which could be very turbulent and destructive, particularly for the mother. The second-born child has a life of fate and destiny, which is probably influenced by the powerful father.

Ketu in the 7th house

There's an attraction for partners who need help, eg, an underdog or outcast in society. Your partner is needy, playing the part of a victim. They may need help, but are reluctant to change and do what's needed. Since you're always the giver, a sense of power and confidence is achieved with the ability to help. There's always something missing in the area of relationships, never bringing fulfillment. The spouse will have very light-colored or unusual eyes. On rare occasions the partner is very spiritual but their detachment may create a sense of distance in the relationship.

The maternal grandmother is very detached, or non-existent, but very perceptive. The second-born child may have emotional or physical problems due to problems with the father.

Rahu in the 8th house

There is an obsessive-compulsive need to be in control, which disturbs marital life. Sexual powers are used to attract sick relationships. Addictions control the life. An inflated sense of power can cause abuse. Surrender is the message that can heal the life.

There is a powerful magnetism and charisma that attracts others. You stand out in a crowd with this power. Financial gains come from others, such as a partner, or from an inheritance.

Ketu in the 8th house

Deep spiritual knowledge, introspection or escape from the material world is the spiritual message for this life. Traumatic events, such as a near-death experience, can transform and change perceptions. Psychic abilities give connection to other dimensions.

Via others taking money from you, or loss of an inheritance, you don't fare well financially from marriage. Others seem to depend on your ability to earn a good living. Fear of abandonment is a core issue that provokes insecure behavior.

Rahu in the 9th house

The father can be very stern, out of control, with an addictive personality. Fanatical views on the world in terms of politics and religion cloud the mind. Travel is impulsive and spontaneous. Problems around travel may bring troubles and loss.

There is an attraction to extremist teachers that have a bias for control, like a cult leader. There is an attraction to cults and non-traditional beliefs.

The spouse shouldn't go into business with a sibling because there's the possibility of a split in the family from corruption or extreme differences in opinion.

Grandchildren may live far away, or else mis-communication with them may drive them away or cause a split.

Ketu in the 9th house

Spirituality is a burning desire and focus throughout the life. Many of life's circumstances lead one to want enlightenment of the soul. The father is not present, physically, mentally or emotionally. There is a deep desire to connect with him for there seems to always be a void or emptiness.

The eternal quest is in finding the truth in all matters. A career in teaching religion or spirituality is possible. Travel to unusual places such as a spiritual pilgrimage brings a feeling of connection.

Grandchildren may have emotional or physical problems. There is disconnection with the spouse's siblings.

Rahu in the 10th house

Drive and power bring success quickly but there are many consequences along the way. Success comes from an unusual career. There is a power that comes from a deep-seated insecurity to prove one's self. The message in childhood was that we are nothing without money, and dedication to hard work is the only way to achieve self-respect and self-worth.

The father may have addictions, such as alcohol, and may treat the mother in inappropriate ways. Family discord plagued early childhood. The mother-in-law is excessive in many ways.

Ketu in the 10th house

A very unusual career is preferred, not confined to an office, where freedom and variety are essential. Something always seems to be missing in the area of work, so changes in career are common. Given this search

45

to find a career that is fulfilling, that quest never seems to be fulfilled. You're forever searching for a career about which you're passionate.

There's a sadness arising from the father's childhood, and a subsequent dissatisfaction with his life. His frustration in achieving his life goals consequently makes you pursue a career helping others.

Rahu in the 11th house

The mother may have been separated from you at birth. There are many influential and powerful people in life that can provide opportunities, all there for the asking. The father is successful and knows people in power. There are connections with people who are in control, the movers and shakers of the community.

Your friends are very materialistic, which has both positive and negative effects. You should be careful of being involved in financial dealings with them.

The partner may have children from a previous marriage. Your first-born child may move far from home, or their marriage may cause problems.

Ketu in the 11th house

Unusual friends and groups stand out as a defining aspect of life. The unique and unconventional types are preferred − underdogs or outcasts in society. Unusual groups, eg, metaphysical or spiritual, are a part of your life. There's a constant yearning to do something of meaning that can help others. Something is always missing until that need to fulfill life with meaning and purpose is complete. Friends cause a drain emotionally and do not reciprocate in kind.

The oldest child will feel a great loss within relationships and marriage, with a tendency to attract those who are troubled.

Rahu in the 12th house

Rahu in the 12th house indicates deep attachments to the material world. Deep-seated fears and secrets control many reactions and responses in life, causing addictions.

There is a fascination with foreigners and foreign lands. Attainment of spiritual powers via concentration and mental conditioning can be used for self-gain.

Secret enemies such as thieves and robbers can attack and invade privacy.

You may have trouble falling asleep, or have nightmares that interrupt your sleep or disturb your peace of mind.

Ketu in the 12th house

Ketu in the 12 house indicates a spiritual search for purpose and meaning. This spiritual quest is never-ending and may always feel like a void that needs to be filled. There is a desire for deep love that is not of this world.

Mystical journeys to foreign lands provide a feeling of freedom and escape. Interest in the unknown motivates your learning about the metaphysical sciences, meditation, and life beyond death.

You may have prophetic dreams. It's productive to keep a dream journal, a window into the subconscious mind whose knowledge transcends our worldly experience.

CHAPTER 7

Dispositors of Rahu and Ketu: Our Karmic Destiny

The next process to be analyzed to give deeper meaning to the past karmas is to refer to the sign dispositors of Rahu and Ketu. There is a pattern associated with these opposite signs therefore certain Karmas are likely for certain groups of individuals.

Here are the patterns of signs:

• Aries/Libra disposited by Mars/Venus

• Taurus/Scorpio disposited by Venus/Mars

• Gemini/Sagittarius disposited by Mercury/Jupiter

• Cancer/Capricorn disposited by Moon/Saturn

• Leo/Aquarius disposited by Sun/Saturn

• Virgo/Pisces disposited by Mercury/Jupiter

So there is a pattern with Mercury/Jupiter, Mars/Venus and Saturn with either the Sun or Moon. These ruling planets always work together. Those with the Venus/Mars rulerships have specific lessons pertaining to relationships, love and money. Relationships are indicated more with Aries/Libra, while money and power are typically Taurus/Scorpio. Meanwhile, the Mercury/Jupiter duo has issues with learning and beliefs, while the Sun and Moon and Saturn have issues with authority and leadership.

The houses in which these planets are located are significant as to the issues and areas of life the individual must experience and learn in this lifetime.

On a deeper level the nakshatras can be very significant in terms of Rahu and Ketu. Of the 27 nakshatras used in Vedic astrology there are three nakshatras ruled by Rahu – Ardra, Swati and Shatabhishak – and three ruled by Ketu – Ashwini, Magha, and Mula. Because they are ruled by the bringers of destiny Rahu and Ketu these nakshatras are considered pivotal.

Just as with the sign dispositors, the nakshatra dispositors can be read in terms of the houses they occupy. The most intense of all the Rahu- and Ketu-ruled nakshatras are Ardra ruled by Rahu and Mula ruled by Ketu. They produce the greatest extremes in tragedy and destruction.

The other opposing nakstratras, with Rahu and Ketu as the rulers in their own sign, are Shatabhishak ruled by Rahu and Magha ruled by Ketu, in opposing signs Aquarius and Leo. Swati ruled by Rahu and Ashwini ruled by Ketu are in opposing signs Libra and Aries. These placements are the most powerful positions for extremes in intellect and intense life's events.

The sign dispositors, which are the key to understanding the karmic destiny of Rahu and Ketu, tell the story of the past and future. In the sections that follow, we can outline the manifestation of what they mean via the house placements.

Note, however, that these are pure indications based only on house attributes. The aspects of other planets to these positions can of course alter the results listed here.

Rahu or Ketu in Aries or Scorpio: Mars is dispositor

"The planet that is the dispositor of Rahu or Ketu indicates the past lessons to be experienced and learned in this life. As Ketu is our past and Rahu is our future together they bring forth our karmic lessons and our destiny. Therefore, they are to be read as one and the same as to their house placements".

Mars as the dispositor of Rahu or Ketu will bring awareness and a sense of purpose to what must be accomplished in this life. This may be uncomfortable but is a part of the growth we're intended to achieve in this life.

With Rahu or Ketu in Aries or Scorpio, Mars is the dispositor, and will therefore exert its influence through the houses as follows:

Mars in the 1st house

There is a tendency to always being on the go. You can never slow down or be still, always needing to move fast, never taking the time to be in the present moment. This can cause impatience and recklessness that may lead to accidents.

The temperament is fiery and focused on your own needs, with a bit of selfishness. This can interfere with relationships, causing contention and fighting.

The karmic lesson here is to learn consideration for others and slow down. Take to heart what others are feeling and saying. Taking these concerns seriously helps issues surrounding relationships.

Mars in the 2nd house

Wealth and money come easily, but a desire to spend money can cause concern and problems in relationships because you don't like being told what to do with your money. You take offence when others try to control you this way.

Family issues are a part of your turmoil, with arguments and fighting from early life. This sets the stage for anger and conflict in married life.

When trying to take charge and be in control, you have a way of saying hurtful things. The need to be in control creates more tension and actually makes you feel more out of control. The gift of speech has been abused in past lives. Therefore, you must think before you speak and use words to heal instead of hurt.

Mars in the 3rd house

Processing information is fast and continual. Traveling is a part of life, expanding awareness. But there is a deep karma to be resolved with siblings.

A sibling is out of control and leaves you angry and upset, but you must address this issue within yourself, and find a way to resolve the anger they stir within you. Learn to accept their ways and don't let them push your buttons with thoughts of how they've hurt you.

Finding your peace with them will heal your past karma. This has been occurring for many lifetimes, and now is the opportunity to heal and resolve this karmic issue once and for all.

Mars in the 4th house

You're seeking a sense of security that you never had in previous lifetimes or even from early life. Situations around the home have always been troubled. There is fear that the family will break up like in your past.

There is a sense that at any minute the rug will be pulled out from underneath you. Operating with a sense of impending fear creates many fear-driven emotions and reactions to life's experiences, sometimes with an overcompensating sense of achievement.

There's a feeling that you must prove yourself, to avoid the sense of helplessness left over from childhood, a time when you had no power to change difficult situations.

There is usually a combative relationship with the mother. Real estate gives security with ownership of expensive real estate.

You must find peace in yourself through accomplishments that empower you. But to heal yourself, you must also empower others. Being secure in yourself means you can give and share success with others, which further strengthens your own sense of security.

Mars in the 5th house

You are gifted intellectually. You have a need to understand the mechanics of everything, from mundane objects, to high tech and their related concepts. You are creative and expressive. This is the house of *poorva punya*, the good karma due to you in this lifetime.

Past good karma, what we carry from past lives, manifests as natural talent. Mars here gives a powerful intellect with great understanding.

The problematic area pertains to children. You may not want kids or literally have trouble conceiving. You'll have issues around children that may consume your life, have difficult kids or be in a situation of not wanting them. A past karmic memory of difficulty with children, possibly death through childbirth, causes fear in this life. Issues involving children are to be healed in this life.

Mars in the 6th house

Health and healing will be a constant theme in your life. Body image can be just one issue you're here to overcome. The desire for perfection is important and you expect others to uphold your ideals. Diets and health fads can consume your life because you feel a sense of urgency to heal on several levels - physical, emotional and mental.

Coworkers and conditions around the workplace can be confrontational. You are here to learn balance with others with a common pursuit. Counseling and helping people will help with your own issues. As you help others, you help yourself, realizing their issues reflect your own.

Mars in the 7th house

Relationships bring upheaval, and trigger emotional issues. Many times, confrontations trigger past feelings of abuse from former lifetimes. The current lesson is to not be a victim.

When you feel someone attacks you, look at what it triggers within you and realize you've attracted this experience. You're not innocent, because there's a part of you that attracts the situation and the aggressive person who attacks you.

When you realize what is within you, the issue will slowly dissolve. Once you relinquish the expectations you hold for your partners, the relationship karma will relax its grip on you. You will have loving and healing relationships, with responsible ownership of your actions.

Mars in the 8th house

A deep and penetrating mind is part of your daily thinking and mental processing. The ability to research and find solutions is a talent. You realize you need to have answers and know the reasons for everything. You'd make a remarkable investigator, detective or researcher.

There's a sense of disgrace and humiliation influencing your life. This is a very humbling experience but through humility you are transformed and changed.

At the core of your being you need to be in control, but you realize you can't control anything. The sense of no control can instill great fear, anxiety and obsessive-compulsive behaviors.

The key is to surrender control, because there is no other option. Many times this can involve addictions and even suicidal tendencies.

A quest for metaphysical knowledge, so long as it's not to control others through black magic or other means, can provide many answers.

Mars in the 9th house

Searching for spiritual meaning in life and truth is the ultimate quest in your life. Your father made life difficult. Karma pertaining to the father makes life challenging.

The ultimate realization in life comes from understanding how the limitations of your learned beliefs affect your outlook on life. Changing our conditioned beliefs can free our minds and allow us greater free will, which in turn can release us from the chains of our past karmas.

Once the mind is opened to accept the laws of nature, this can bring a new awareness and freedom of thinking, in which your thoughts are no longer controlled by the past conditioning of family, culture or even politics.

Mars in the 10th house

The need to be in power and have a fulfilling purposeful career is a part of your drive and ambition throughout life. Karmas from a past life lead you to find your life's calling early in life. You establish your sense of self-worth through the success of your work. In childhood a situation inspired you to find a successful career that would lead to a life of fulfillment through recognition and honors.

You will succeed in business with an innate desire to lead. You will not settle for mediocre positions because you aspire to and attain top positions, never stopping in your quest for honors, accolades and awards. This position can give fame and public recognition.

The lesson here is to understand that true power means helping others. Your most satisfying achievement, giving you a true sense of purpose, will come from sharing your knowledge and empowering others.

Mars in the 11th house

There is an innate desire to be heard by others. You wish to share your desires, hopes, and dreams with friends. The need to communicate with others is an essential part of life. When you have an idea, you feel the need to bounce it off others to achieve a sense of credibility.

But somehow there appears to be an unexpected backlash of contention from friends. Out of this response you sometimes feel attacked and misunderstood, with feelings of jealousy from others.

You're here to heal your issues regarding a friend who seems too competitive. The key to resolving this problem is to understand that you attract those who mirror your inner being, and thus end up blaming the friends you reflect. When you're too much alike, you find yourselves in competition, and become repelled. Instead of being insulted, find agreement in common ground, resolve your conflicts and recognize in the threatened friends your similarities.

The karma described here may also refer to a situation with an older sibling.

Mars in the 12th house

There's a deep-seated desire to uncover the injustices of the past. Unconsciously the past controls many of your outbursts of repressed anger. There may be sleep disturbances or vivid and unnerving dreams. This is due to unsettled karmas from a past life.

Because of deep-seated resentments from the past, new resentments are created in this lifetime. Secret enemies appear out of nowhere to invoke the injustices of the past. They're here to teach you the ultimate lesson, leading you from suffering to freedom.

In this lifetime you need to recognize the inner anger that brings to the surface the reactions of a victim in response to injustice. This means you can no longer blame others or outside circumstances for your life's predicaments.

By taking charge and realizing you have a part in the apparent injustices affecting you, you can finally take responsibility for your actions, acknowledging your part in this resulting karma.

Victims never get anywhere if they always blame others. Rather than giving away your power to change, recognize your role in attracting predators, and use this awareness to resolve your dilemma.

Ketu or Rahu in Taurus or Libra: Venus is dispositor

Venus as the dispostor of Ketu will reveal the past karma, issues and experiences that will lead us to spiritual liberation from our past. The gifts and talents brought in with Ketu from a past life are already developed, therefore not challenging and will seem uninteresting, because it was already completed. But these gifts lead the way to new developments to be accomplished in this lifetime represented by Rahu.

With Ketu or Rahu in Taurus or Libra, Venus is the dispositor, and will therefore exert its influence through the houses as follows:

Venus in the 1st house

Venus reflects our power to attract and be in relationships. In the 1st house it gives a refined sense of poise and grace. You have acquired social skills that are innate, not taught in this lifetime. You are a peacekeeper, always making sure your partner is well taken care of.

With a sense of style, you are gifted with beauty, and are appreciated and loved. Your attractiveness brings many suitors, resulting in many relationship opportunities. The partner will provide you many gifts and pleasures.

Good karma is achieved from past fulfilling relationships. This is your blessing for being the caretaker in many lifetimes before.

Venus in the 2nd house

Wealth and prosperity are the products of an innate generosity from previous lifetimes. The home and family are refined and give a sense of security. The family is well off or at least provided a secure childhood environment.

Your voice is pleasing and you speak kind words, thanks to encouragement and respect given you as a child. There may be a gift of singing as your voice is sweet and beautiful.

Your attitude is generous and optimistic due to the past karmas of sophistication and good cultural education.

Venus in the 3rd house

Learning and education in the arts come naturally because these are innate qualities that were fully developed in the past.

You have a gift for all forms of communication, especially writing. Literary skills are instinctive and the way they're presented comes across with ease and confidence.

Your hearing is extremely acute, and you have an intuitive love of music that could well manifest as musical talent.

Siblings are a blessing for they were associated with you in a meaningful way during a past life. You'll remain close throughout this lifetime.

Venus in the 4th house

You're likely to have a beautiful home full of tasteful decorations or art. This is a gift of good karma because the 4th house is the house of happiness.

Due to your nurturing and care as a provider in a previous life, you've been rewarded with a happy home that brings both security and contentment. Helping others achieve a sense of security and love confirms these rewards.

A love for beautiful surroundings and a sense of color, design and refinement were developed in previous lifetimes. There is a quality of royalty from the past that makes for a beautiful home life. Even the landscaping is impeccable.

To be surrounded by beauty makes the soul happy because of its remembrances of the past. Security comes from a loving family and nurturing mother.

Venus in the 5th house

Blessings are given through the support and happiness from children. The children will be pleasing and beautiful. This is a desire manifested from previous lifetimes.

As the house of *poorva punya*, meaning good karma due to you in this lifetime, Venus here gives a great mind and the power of creativity. This reflects a talent developed in previous lifetimes that were generally very artistic.

This is the house of entertainment and fun, therefore many people with this placement have the innate need to express themselves creatively. You may be a performer, athlete, writer, artist, or musician.

Venus in the 6th house

The gift here is health, because in past lives and in your early life you took exceptional care of your body, through diet and exercise. The payoff now is a strong, healthy beautiful body that lasts a lifetime.

You're lucky in the area of employment, falling into the right job early that pays off in the long run. Lifelong friendships are formed through work, and even your employees become friends.

Careers that serve and help or heal others give fulfillment and empowerment. Your quest is always to counsel and heal, thus creating more good karma for the future. After early struggles, children give security through their wealth.

Venus in the 7th house

Partnerships are the most important aspect of your life. Venus here is intense, indicating a charming and attractive partner, thus attracting others into your space.

In previous lifetimes you were the one with many who desired you before.

The focus and attention is on working out this issue of love and marriage. This time around you are learning to trust. If you are mistrustful of your partner, you'll find reasons not to trust. But if you learn to trust, your partner will be trustworthy.

Your partner will give you gifts, money, and even great wealth if you can overcome the past karmas.

Venus in the 8th house

Your gift is deep awareness and intuitive sight. You may be overly obsessive when it comes to matters of love and romance. There was a major betrayal from a previous lifetime that has caused deep suspicions.

Your sensuality and sexuality are overpowering, and you have powers of attraction with sexual charisma that can attract all kinds. Be careful who you allow into your life

Money comes from others, either through marriage or inheritance. This is the settlement of many karmic dues. You've paid the price in previous lives to acquire this payback. But the money comes through great difficulty and loss, and hardly brings happiness.

Venus in the 9th house

Blessings are gained through the father or a teacher who brings guidance and light into your life. You seem to meet the right people at the right time throughout life.

You're gifted with money and wealth from a past life. This is a major sign of luck. In reality it is more than luck, it comes from very pious deeds in the past.

Your innate spiritual beliefs are strong, with a sense of great devotion, due to the development of your spirituality before. You have a great love of the Divine. Therefore, you're always protected, especially when you travel.

Grandchildren will bring benefits and blessings into your life because you were deeply connected in a past life, probably a parent before.

Venus in the 10th house

You'll make a name for yourself through your career because you developed a talent that can be used in this life.

Attuned to your social standing and presence in the world, you're polished and confident. Your sense of fashion and culture help you stand out in a crowd.

Acclaim for your creative talents in this lifetime is due to a developed appreciation in these areas through previous lifetimes.

Creative design, fashion, writing, arts, and music come to you with ease. You could easily pursue a career in these or related fields.

Venus in the 11th house

Many groups or organizations will benefit from your talents. You have the power to direct and lead others in a graceful fashion. Skilled in politics, you find common ground within groups.

You were quite the leader in a previous lifetime, helping others achieve their goals. Now you achieve your goals through the cooperation of others who'll bring benefits to you.

Charitable groups are your passion, and you provide benefits and healing to those who are less fortunate.

Organizations that promote the arts benefit from your gatherings and fundraising. You can raise money for, and interest in, schools and education, especially concerning the performing arts, music and museums.

Venus in the 12th house

Venus is the only planet that picks up strength in the 12th house, and this often indicates wealth.

Great wealth is due to good karma with relationships within families. You gave time and money to charities in past lives. You still have a generous spirit from past lifetimes.

Through understanding the power of forgiveness in this life, there will be a letting-go of past resentments. This is a placement for healing relationships. You'll come to understand where you went wrong, and gain the power to heal through love.

Rahu or Ketu in Gemini or Virgo: Mercury is dispositor

This configuration indicates a quest for knowledge and learning. Learning can come through education, communications of all kinds, travel and contacts with other people.

The need to connect with others is an essential part of this world, and often consumes our lives. We're all in constant communication with others, sharing out thoughts and ideas. Our desire to relate and connect to others makes our life fulfilling. We spend all of our waking hours in communication via phones, computers, TV, and radio.

Our relationship with others teaches us about ourselves. Our lives would be meaningless without our ability to connect and relate to others. We all have the need to share our lives and experiences.

The air houses, which pertain to communications, are associated with the 3rd, 7th, and 11th houses. The 3rd house is brothers and sisters, 7th is marriage, and the 11th is friends. These involve our primary relationships (siblings, partners, friends) with whom we need to share our ideas.

If we consider Rahu as the future and our need to grow through these unchartered waters, Mercury as dispositor provides an understanding of the karma inherent in individuals who are vested in their need to communicate, learn, travel and explore the world through connections to others.

With Rahu or Ketu in Gemini or Virgo, Mercury is the dispositor, and will therefore exert its influence through the houses as follows:

Mercury in the 1st house

This is the lifetime to travel and see the world. You need to express yourself through adventure, for you were an explorer in previous lives. You feel especially connected to people from foreign places, and are well versed with other cultures. Multicultural, you strive to learn other languages.

All forms of communication with others are important to you. You may spend lots of time on your phone, via Skype or Facetime, to connect with friends in foreign lands.

A great blessing of Mercury in the 1st house is agelessness. You're eternally youthful. Since you relate well with the younger generation, you may find your partners and associates becoming younger.

You've always wanted to write a book, mainly because you have so much to say and your life is never boring. This could be a significant goal for this lifetime.

Always gathering new information, you read, listen to audios, and seek to develop new skills through classes or tutorials. Your mind never shuts off; you love to learn.

Another thing that interests you is gossip, scandals and conspiracy theories, anything to uncover secrets.

Mercury in the 2nd house

As a child you began speaking early, and from that point on you never stopped. Your family encouraged you to speak and may have inspired you to learn another language. An affinity for languages was a trait developed in previous lifetimes.

Always expressing yourself, you're the first to lunge for the phone when it rings. You spend way too much time on the phone, and would always rather speak then use a text to communicate.

Because you have a way with words, you should develop your public speaking skills. You're often the one who is appointed to be the spokesperson on your job. This is an excellent role for someone whose life thrives on constant communication. You're a natural teacher and translator.

Mercury in the 3rd house

This is a perfect position for a writer. You have a gift for the written word. You can master all forms of communication skills, even related technologies.

You're a perpetual student, always searching for that missing piece of information to solve a puzzle and complete the picture. But the more you learn, the more you realize you don't know.

Since you're so expressive with words and love to learn, you'll probably end up teaching in some capacity. This is a gift you brought from other lifetimes.

In constant movement, you're always traveling, perhaps spending a lot of time commuting to work, or even travel for a living.

Vastly creative, you have many talents and love performing. You may write music, articles, codes, poems or contracts. Your business could also involve advertising.

You love to make things and have a gift for using your hands. You're good with craft-work and can fix most anything around the house.

Mercury in the 4th house

The home offers many gadgets, computers, books, and games, all to promote a learning environment. Your mother may be intelligent, and does all she can to provide educational opportunities.

It's important for you to achieve a college degree, perhaps even a master's or doctorate. Education is held in high esteem by your family.

The parents may uproot the family many times, searching for the best place to call home. You're always looking for a home in a better place, but never really feel settled. This is a carry-over from other lives living as a gypsy.

You never feel attached to the home and can also leave the past behind, which is one of your best attributes – to never dwell on the past.

Mercury in the 5th house

You're graced with common sense, high intelligence, and a philosophical mind. You're pragmatic and love to teach. Intellectual gifts and talents come from previous lives.

Your mind is very adaptable, and you can learn almost any subject. The right and left brain, cognitive and creative sides, are equally developed. Creativity comes naturally, whether it be through artistic or mechanical skills. This is a common placement for someone who writes books.

Mercury here gives great intellectual capacity, even in metaphysical sciences, especially astrology. People will come to you for advice and guidance. You could be a consultant for powerful people.

This is a good position for investors and investments, gives acumen in the stock market. Children will be highly intelligent and extremely practical, thus ensuring their success.

Mercury in the 6th house

Skills in counseling and healing come courtesy of their development in past lives, for this is the house that pertains to health. This suggests a need to heal or nurture others back to health.

It indicates those who like to help others, eg, nurses, doctors, therapists, acupuncturists, dieticians, naturopaths, yoga instructors, athletic teachers, and health store personnel. Other fields of service are also held in high regard, entailing anything to do with food or drink service, eg, restaurant, bar, hotel or airline attendants.

Although Mercury here indicates someone meant to be in field of health or service, it also implies a love of animals and their care in this life.

Mercury in the 7th house

Partnerships are the main focus in life. You feel you can't prosper without the recognition and support of a partner. Your sense of self-worth is reflected in how your partner views you. But always seeking the support of a partner can be energy-consuming.

You feel most connected by having great communication with your loved one. Rapport and partnership are continuous throughout the day. Sometimes you feel connected through mental telepathy, and can finish each other's sentences.

You need a partner who is intelligent and communicative, with a keen sense of humor. These are key elements required in your relationship.

Although it may seem a bit needy, the connection with a like-minded partner gives a sense of completion and is essential for a life that feels whole. This is the karma to relate or commune with someone on an intellectual level.

Mercury in the 8th house

Mercury is the only planet that prospers in the 8th house and indicates using the intelligence to research.

You have the mind of an investigator or scientist, always probing for information and secrets. Scandals are uncovered and mysteries revealed. You have a gift for understanding concepts beyond this world.

This placement can indicate an affinity for metaphysics, since the deeper meanings of life are revealed via this position. Metaphysical or occult knowledge arises from past lives.

Psychics and mediums have a natural talent to investigate other worlds and spirits. There's an innate interest in the unknown, and things beyond this world.

Understanding the process of death and communication with the dead are gifts of Mercury in the 8th house.

Mercury in the 9th house

Travel to foreign places activates the mind to learn more about different cultures. This placement inspires the mind in spiritual and philosophical ways. It may encourage you to participate in spiritual pilgrimages, thus learning more about religion and spirituality.

You gravitate to higher learning and never want to leave school. You're the one to pursue higher education, to become a professor, always in academia.

Guidance comes from teachers and gurus, as well as your father who's likely an esteemed and intelligent man.

You'll explore the world, study many forms of spirituality and eventually become your own teacher. You inspire others to embrace higher learning, education, spirituality and travel, just as you did in previous lives.

Mercury in the 10th house

An entrepreneur you're always searching for the perfect business model. You learn through others and will end up teaching people how to be as successful as yourself. A fulfilling career is a gift, as it was in previous lifetimes.

You have the ability to take on many different businesses, and pride yourself in managing at least two at the same time.

Business will involve travel and all forms of communication, including social media, since your business may reflect significant involvement in the world of advertising.

Computers, apps, and inventions are the name of the game. You never shut down from working all the time. Your ideas are always on the cutting edge, involving whatever is new and appeals to the younger generations.

Mercury in the 11th house

Connecting to large groups and institutions is a talent that gets you into many up-and-coming businesses. You have the capacity to work with many people, and will succeed in a business that is international.

Social skills are your gift, since you're diverse and love connecting people from around the world. You have many friends who come together with a purpose, uniting and healing differences between cultures.

Since you have a talent for speaking to large groups, this can catapult you into leadership positions in corporations. Your respect for humanity originates from spiritual work achieved in other lifetimes.

Your friends introduce you to the connections you need to find a career that opens you to international trade and communications.

You may have an intellectual elder sibling that is a source of pride for you.

Mercury in the 12th house

You're connected to foreign people who inspire and teach you about the diversity of different cultures. Travel and understanding others is your passion. This is a part of your destiny, to learn in this lifetime, since you were an international messenger before.

Given your love for movies, your imagination is ripe for the film industry. You have great ideas for movies and documentaries. You're interested in anything to do with outer space or fantasy worlds beyond our own. Mystical dreams give the power to perceive the future.

A career with the travel or shipping industry, anything to do with connecting people and places worldwide, is appropriate for you. This could also play out through ideas involving media, whether advertising or entertainment.

You have a natural desire to connect with the divine forces of nature, ultimately finding oneness with all.

Ketu or Rahu in Sagittarius or Pisces: Jupiter is dispositor

Ketu or Rahu in a Jupiter-ruled sign indicates a quest and burning desire for truth and spirituality. The focus here regards life's mission as related to beliefs, philosophy and the meaning of life.

Jupiter is the planet of freedom and opportunities, and its placement opens doors to the future from the gifts of the past.

With Ketu or Rahu in Sagittarius or Pisces, Jupiter is the dispositor, and will therefore exert its influence through the houses as follows:

Jupiter in the 1st house

There is an innate confidence that comes courtesy of past accomplishments. The stature will be robust, with a strong presence in the physical demeanor.

There may be an air of righteousness, an all-knowing attitude, about you because you've been a leader in philosophical and religious groups in previous lives.

You're confident in your beliefs and can be pushy in convincing others.

You command respect because you were deeply respected by many before. Leadership roles come readily and you seem to fall into positions easily without much effort because of service to others in lifetimes before.

There is the tendency for excess and over-expansion, since things came easily without restriction before.

Jupiter in the 2nd house

Wealth and prosperity manifest easily in this life due to a great generosity in previous lives. In past lifetimes the family was well off and respected and in this life they are born into a similar situation. This gives a sense of accomplishment with many opportunities.

You're well-spoken and find it easy to express yourself. High morals are a personal attribute. You inspire and speak to others on how truthfulness will always lead to the greatest accomplishments.

An inner security instills a sense of happiness in this life. You're able to help those in need just as you did in former lifetimes.

Jupiter in the 3rd house

Learning and education come easily because this was your focus in previous lifetimes. Open-minded, you're seeking freedom, and this means finding the truth. You are a philosopher finding ways to unite people through spiritual reality.

The main mission of this life comes through the written word. There is a deep sense of purpose to expose the reality and meaning of life. A book needs to come out in this lifetime.

Travel is an important component of your life because you need to experience different ways of perceiving the world. You know there are many paths to truth and yours can be the voice that helps others with this realization.

You have a love of culture and are interested in diverse ways of living. You feel the need to bring cultures together to appreciate our essential unity.

Jupiter in the 4th house

Your upbringing was secure and there was a spiritual element present in the family that kept them together. You always feel good when you're at home because of a sense of security that was instilled in pervious lifetimes.

There's a certain honor and prestige that was imparted in previous lifetimes and you feel that family ties should never be broken. Your mother taught the importance of family and upholding certain values and virtues.

Real estate and property are important, with the possibility of an inheritance that comes from property. The home is a safe haven for you.

Security comes from a family whose foundation is education and positive values. You are fortunate in this life and your good karma is to receive the blessings of a good family.

Jupiter in the 5th house

You are blessed with high intelligence and a deep sense of spirituality. This blessing gives leadership positions in which your advice is sought. You were an advisor to the elite before.

Because you were a truth seeker before and gave guidance to powerful people, seeking the deeper meaning and purpose of life comes naturally to you. This indicates great spiritual or metaphysical knowledge achieved in previous lifetimes.

Children can be your teachers but sometimes Jupiter in the 5th house denies children. They can be your greatest blessing, bestowing love and happiness.

In this lifetime you're here to teach the truth. There will be many opportunities to share your ideas and guidance with others.

Jupiter in the 6th house

You have the power to heal others because you were a healer before and are meant to use these powers again. It's natural for you to counsel and help others solve their problems because in previous lifetimes you were a master at finding solutions.

There is an affinity for healing through food. You love to cook and know how to use food for optimum nutrition.

Blessings will come through your extended family – aunts and uncles. Children are a meaningful part of your life as you have deep karmic ties from previous lifetimes.

You will have all the support and help you need throughout life due to all the support and help you gave to others in former lifetimes. You were a healer and now you will be healed, physically, mentally, emotionally and spiritually.

Jupiter in the 7th house

You are blessed with the encouragement of a partner who can help you. Life is easy now because you have the love and support you need. This is because you were the one to provide support in pervious lifetimes.

The partner may be in a powerful position, admired by many. You can't be jealous. Let them lead the way and you'll be taken care of throughout life.

Your partner has a lot to teach you if you choose to listen. They may be a bit boastful but their intentions are always good.

The security of a partnership can help unlock opportunities for a fulfilling life. This lifetime is more about you lending the support so that your partner can shine in this life. The roles were reversed before.

Jupiter in the 8th house

You'll be taken care of in this lifetime through the money and wealth of others. An inheritance will come through family or marriage. Because you gave so much to the family before, now is your time to receive.

Deep intuition and psychic ability are your gifts from previous lifetimes as you were a prophet shedding light on the truth.

The power to foresee future events makes you uneasy, but this gift can give hope and a sense of security. Thanks to your good intentions, you've acquired spiritual knowledge. You're here in this lifetime to share your vision with future generations.

Connections to spiritual and mystical realms can give you the power to manifest good in this world.

Jupiter in the 9th house

Spiritual knowledge and teaching were a way of life in your previous lifetimes. You were once the guru, philosopher and professor, and cannot be anything else. You love teaching and inspiring others through your philosophies.

Your presence can be a bit daunting to others because you're overly confident in your beliefs. Justice and truthfulness is your way of life and those afraid of the light may shun you.

The father who was your teacher in previous lifetimes has now resolved to be your student. He is a man of virtue and has given you opportunities that have empowered your life.

Regardless of your position in life, you share your philosophy and belief in unity and understanding, a message with a purpose.

Jupiter in the 10th house

Having been a leader in your past-life career, you're given opportunities again for success in this lifetime. Since you helped other people achieve their goals, now you're given the same chances you offered others. Empowering others in the business world enhances your position and brings wealth.

Opportunities came from your children in a previous life. In this life you'll bring them into one of your enterprises.

Honors and prestige are bestowed through your career because you have been an honorable business person with integrity. You'll be rewarded in this lifetime with a meaningful profession.

Jupiter in the 11th house

Your connection to influential people from previous lifetimes brings opportunities in this life. You gave your time and resources to your friends and now you have their support.

Hugely popular, you're surrounded and supported by many. You share a bond with friends who have the same feelings and ideals. Generosity flows both ways in many dealings with your associates.

Your sense of trust in friendships and relationships paved the way for your children. Through your role modeling, they will become honorable and good-hearted adults.

Your oldest sibling set a good example and has given you opportunities and protection throughout life.

Jupiter in the 12th house

Generosity is a part of your nature. Due to your kindness in your past life you are given many riches in this life. Charities and organizations for the betterment of mankind benefit from your efforts to heal problems plaguing this world.

The world is a better place due to your work, for which you receive the benefits of good karma. As you give you continue to receive in this life, just as you gave to so many others before.

There's a deep spiritual connection to worlds beyond your present existence. You're able to connect to the collective unconscious when you sleep, and are given the gift of prophecy through vivid dreams.

Being connected to the Divine, you might never take the world's suffering as seriously as others because you've seen it's merely an illusion like the rest of our existence.

Rahu or Ketu in Cancer: Moon is dispositor

With Rahu or Ketu in Cancer, the Moon as dispositor reflects a deep emotional current from the past. Feelings and impressions are connected to experiences from early childhood or past lives. It's hard to break patterns due to this connection. Many are predisposed to past conditioning and feel things at a gut level.

Wherever the Moon is in a chart will generally indicate where the most fluctuation or changes will occur in your life. The Moon represents the mind or consciousness and its placement is of vital importance because this is where the mind's awareness is focused throughout life.

You're tuned in and have an appreciation for the nurturing instinct. Your gift is to connect on a devotional level to the essence of the Divine mother for protection.

With Rahu or Ketu in Cancer, the Moon is the dispositor, and will therefore exert its influence through the houses as follows:

Moon in the 1st house

You're very sensitive to the environment, and you're affected by smells, tastes, temperature, lights and color. You may even be overly sensitive to pollutants in the air, therefore especially vulnerable to pollen allergies. Even certain foods and medicines can have reverse reactions.

You pick up the feelings of others and absorb negative emotions like a sponge. Water is a great healer for you, so taking baths with salts and essential oils can cleanse the auric field where other's emotions have attached to you.

As a nurturer, you're surrounded by people who'd like to absorb your healing energy, but make sure they're people you care for who can reciprocate. You're here to protect and heal others emotionally in this lifetime.

Moon in the 2nd house

Childhood was fraught with many emotional ups and downs where nothing seemed stable and secure. That established a sense of insecurity wherein money matters were problematic in terms of having a secure income. It seemed to be all or nothing.

The more you worry about finances, the less they seem available. This is a deep-seated unconscious fear that was initiated in childhood. Fear of poverty keeps you in this predicament. Healing a mind fixated on this previous lack of security will solve this dilemma.

You're here to develop a sense of security in family and financial matters. This is the karma attributed to your fears surrounding money. Stability may seem like water passing through your hands, but once you realize this is only a fear and not a reality, the foundation is established to let healing begin.

Moon in the 3rd house

The Moon in the 3rd house usually means you're youngest of your family. Either that, or the youngest sibling has many insecurities.

An attachment to feelings from the past keeps you stuck in reoccurring patterns that you want to escape. These patterns are a continuation from a past life.

Your hearing is acute, so noises and music have a deep effect on your emotions. You sense and feel what others are thinking. Being a good listener, others come to you with their problems.

Learning is fun for you, so you can make it a game. The mind is always searching for stimulating information. Self-expression is an essential part of your nature. The arts of all kinds appeal to you — writing, painting, dancing, music and acting.

Gossip can get you in trouble because anytime you speak of others it always seems to come back to you. Participating in gossip is irresistible but never serves a good purpose.

Moon in the 4th house

There is a deep insecurity that originated in childhood due to instability within the family. Erratic events destabilized your peace of mind. Changes in residence caused a disconnection without a sense of safety.

Your parents were not present, either physically or emotionally. The mother is perceptive and sensitive emotionally, but is unpredictable and deeply insecure.

You're intelligent, with an impressionable mind and a photographic memory that makes schooling and education come easily. You have a talent for mimicry and impersonations. You have a mind that never forgets, but some things are better forgotten, for to dwell on the past never helps the future.

Moon in the 5th house

Highly intelligent, you're constantly working on new projects to improve your life and gain security. You are creative and inventive, and want to use your ideas to help other people.

Love has a different meaning for you, based on values of loyalty and commitment. You love so deeply that you can't imagine spreading your love. As in previous lives, it is a focus of your current life.

Children are important to you but since you feel the need to focus your love, you limit them to only one or two.

Your innate wisdom and understanding of life's experiences attracts others who seek your guidance and advice. You are often placed in advisory positions.

Moon in the 6th house

Your purpose in life is to help others, so you typically seek a career that allows you to be of service. Helping others is the most gratifying. This may come from a career in health care, food service, counseling, or hospitality.

Being extremely sensitive to food, you are attuned to the flavors and finer aspects of culinary experience. Nurturing others with food and drink comes naturally.

You're here to understand, learn and heal yourself – body, mind and spirit. This may come through your work to help others.

Your mother's family, aunts and uncles are important and have a great influence on you. You had close connections with them in previous lives.

Moon in the 7th house

Relationships are your focus, because you want to learn how to acquire and maintain a long-lasting one, having experienced so much unpredictability in past lives.

You put a lot of faith in your partner, but when your high expectations aren't fulfilled, you become distraught. The lesson here is to let go of unrealistic expectations, which inevitably led to disappointment.

As you nurture and care for others, you're hurt when your feelings aren't reciprocated, which creates resentments. Learn not to take things so personally, because this is the key to healing your relationship issues in this life.

Moon in the 8th house

Life seems to be difficult when starting out. Your childhood was troubled by problems that affected your mother. She had great difficulties in her life and may seem to have passed on the emotional torment.

The anguish of feeling inferior casts a spell on your ability to succeed, but the main lesson is to avoid letting the past control your future. Don't look back. Accept that you can't undo the apparently-fated events that seem to have scarred you. Now that you're in charge, focus on future success.

Feelings of shame and humiliation cast shadows on your life. This is primarily from circumstances you have no control over. Focus on the things you can control, and take initiative and responsibility to create a different life. This will induce the transformational healing you're here to grow through.

Moon in the 9th house

Devotion to a spiritual path gives you the security and life you were meant to experience. You're confused by unpredictable and unexplainable difficulties but you can change direction by changing your belief system. You question truth and religion constantly, because it never seems to be clear or make sense.

Throughout life you observed many hypocritical role models. To say one thing and do another was the norm, so you questioned the validity of any teacher, parent or spiritual teacher.

Your mind is open to multi-cultural ways of understanding. Exposure to different beliefs helps broaden your outlook to see the world and consciousness in a new light. This realization was set in motion from previous lives.

Moon in the 10th house

Career and social recognition are important to you. Your drive to achieve puts you in the public eye. You'll be well known or famous in your field.

In this life you're here to overcome your insecurities concerning work. Although you tend to over-dramatize situations, you're here to cooperate with others rather than tell them what to do. There are issues around women in the work place, especially with those who are your superiors.

Your career success is how you measure your life, image and purpose. In this life you're here to shine. You've made a name for yourself in previous lifetimes, and now you're granted the opportunity for achievement and success.

Moon in the 11th house

A love of humanity and the care of others makes you active in groups and organizations. You have many associates but keep your emotional distance. You can't tolerate wasting time on superficial friendships.

Organizations that help people and uplift the community are where you give your heart and soul, but on a deep level you don't like opening your heart.

Your detachment goes back to injustices you experienced in former lives. You're here to heal the injustices of others who forsook you in the past. By doing good for the community you feel you are righting wrongs. Ultimately, this touches you at a personal level. Only when you're able to open your heart to others will you heal the deep-seated issue from the past.

Older siblings are on the same level as your associates, where it's a struggle to truly open your heart and heal the relationship.

Moon in the 12th house

The past has an emotional hold on you, and you're consumed with healing past hurts. But the best way to process the past is to accept things for the way they are. You can't change the past or the people who've hurt you, so you must learn acceptance. Once you're no longer plagued by these emotional upsets, you'll be free.

Your mother had deep emotional ties to you in previous lifetimes, and you're here to heal and release that attachment. Glimpses of the past emerge through dreams. Keep a dream journal and re-read it at the time of the full moon to get a better perspective on your unconscious and its clues on how to heal the past.

Intuition and psychic abilities are a great gift from past lives, and if used positively will give guidance throughout life. You have profound insights.

You're generous to a fault and feel the need to give to anyone in need. Charities and organizations that heal are a part of your life.

Rahu or Ketu in Leo: Sun is dispositor

Rahu or Ketu in Leo concerns issues around authority and leadership. Relationships with bosses, the father and teachers can be challenging and lessons to heal the ego will emerge.

Your leadership and loyalty will be realized through the vast understanding of the past. This will develop your position and power in the world.

With Rahu or Ketu in Leo, the Sun is the dispositor, and will therefore exert its influence through the houses as follows:

Sun in the 1st house

You are confident and have a keen self-regard, sometimes tending to glorify your sense of importance. Your radiance attracts many admirers. The real test is whether you can prevent your ego from consuming and taking over your mission.

As a leader you're put in a position to give guidance and direct the masses who can't think for themselves. The lesson for you is to lead without ego and realize you're to give support.

You're a spiritual warrior, finding your path through turbulent times and helping others with a mission. The test of time arises via adoring fans who may divert your purpose and destroy your mission. In previous lifetimes you were distracted by the ego, but now you know the Divine path.

Sun in the 2nd house

Your mission was clear, ever since childhood when you were given heavy responsibilities. You felt like a failure trying to meet the expectations of your father and family. In previous lifetimes you were unsuccessful in supporting your family but now you're given a second chance.

Finances are a key element in upholding your commitment to the family. You struggle to maintain your honor by providing security to your family. Money is a sore spot because you feel it demanded too much attention in the past.

Being concerned with the status quo, and keeping up with the neighbors, is a problem. Buying things to appear more successful creates stress that will be your eventual downfall. Be true to yourself and let go of the superficial pretenses that prevent you from enjoying your family.

Sun in the 3rd house

You may have deep karmic ties with a sibling. You judge yourself by constant comparison. Due to a past life of constant competition, you always feel inferior. In this life you must now come to terms with the fact that you're equal, and can complement and support each another.

Your constant drive to outdo others in sports or education overshadows the gains you might receive through these activities. You have to let go of your competitive edge.

You have a unique ability to express yourself, and others will listen if you become humbler in your expression. You're here for sharing your ideas, not outdoing others. Although you harbor a memory of previous lifetimes where you competed with siblings, this karmic past must be released.

Sun in the 4th house

Security through a happy home life is what you're unconsciously searching for. This manifests as looking for approval from your mother, who perhaps didn't know how to protect or nurture you.

You find yourself seeking security in land, real estate, money, and love. But true happiness comes from the connection within yourself. Finding security through your own sense of yourself is what's required in this lifetime.

Constant searching for something you lack is a core issue. But you already have what you need. You've found your true home. All issues around love are healed once you realize your home offers the peace and love you need within your heart. Your family will support and love you for this.

Sun in the 5th house

You're a natural leader and will be put in positions of authority to give guidance to those who wield power. In essence you're the one who wields power through others. You are the ultimate advisor.

In previous lifetimes you abused this authority but now you're given a second chance. See it as an opportunity to give guidance rather than take control, to offer true spiritual counsel without ego involvement.

Powerful children can uplift and guide your life. This placement usually denotes a powerful male child, a special gift from a previous life. Your children open your heart to give unconditional love.

This is a placement indicating good past karma wherein many gifts and talents are bestowed on you. Take them but give back to the world in a heart-felt message of love. You are very blessed!

Sun in the 6th house

Your generous spirit grants you constitutional strength and health. You've helped so many in a past life that you're rewarded with good health and the power to heal others. This could be physical healing or in some other line of service. Your heart and soul thrive in helping others.

Health, diet, nutrition and exercise are important. Your good health gives physical strength, stamina, ambition and a competitive edge. You rarely get sick because your powerful immune system wards off disease. You're a role model and an inspiration for others to attend to their health.

You love all aspects of nature, including animals. You know the emotional healing power of owning, loving and caring for a pet.

Sun in the 7th house

Your spouse is the heart and soul of your life, but they may demand the center of attention. To have a happy and healthy relationship, you must surrender to their needs. In former lifetimes you controlled the relationship, but now you must let them have the lead. This isn't easy, since your natural tendencies stem from your previous role.

Your spouse may have an overwhelming ego, and now is their time to shine. You may have to stand in their shadow as they take the limelight.

As you surrender you'll grow within, as is your purpose. As you give of yourself your partner will in turn love you and give back more than you gave up.

Sun in the 8th house

Your light comes through recognizing your faults, a hard thing for you to do. In your past life, you were consumed with power and ego, but now you have to admit your faults.

Deep issues of shame and humiliation concern the father. This may be very difficult to come to terms with. Acknowledging the things you've denied for many lifetimes can be devastating, but surrender is the ticket to freedom.

Many addictions stem from fears of the unknown buried in your consciousness. But surrender will enable a powerful transformation, and the release of burdens carried over many lifetimes. In essence, this is the death of the ego, which bares your soul and brings enlightenment.

Sun in the 9th house

You have a powerful sense of leadership although your spiritual beliefs have convinced you that your way is the only way to the truth. Your ego will be humbled through exposure to life experiences that challenge your righteous beliefs.

As a conqueror on a spiritual path in previous lifetimes, you threw your weight around and hurt others under the guise of the "know it all" philosopher and teacher. You abused your power to guide others but now you'll come to understand your brand of spiritual truth will not bring you the happiness you seek.

You must learn to surrender to others and know that you don't have all the answers. You'll continue to be exposed to injustice and harsh judgment. But until you listen and become the student willing to learn, you'll be beaten down by your supposed truth. With your surrender, truth and happiness can be achieved through love and understanding.

Sun in the 10th house

Power, prestige, and leadership positions manifest easily. You shine in positions of power and are esteemed in your role as a commander. You were a great achiever even in your past life and still have the gift to lead. There's more for you to accomplish in this lifetime.

Your ability to out-shine others in the workplace will attract jealousy, and because you can't take orders from others, you need to run your own business.

You've achieved greatness from previous lifetimes and deserve the recognition you acquire. The only prerequisite is that you never abuse this power by degrading others. Your mission is to exercise leadership by empowering people.

In leadership roles, your challenge is to grant power and share your success with others. This will promise even more good karma in future lives.

Sun in the 11th house

Your ability to lead and empower others in organizations shines through because you were a powerhouse in previous lifetimes. You'll acquire great riches in this life because you were a giver of honors and wealth before.

Your previous lives involved humanitarian efforts, so now you're the recipient of that which you gave yourself to before. Political efforts are now on your agenda, so you strive to help humanity, creating even better karmas for the next life.

The men in your family exert valiant leadership representing values of honor, virtue and loyalty. To have such traits role-modeled is a true gift. Use your good fortune to extend a hand. Help heal humanity's problems and your life will be enriched.

Sun in the 12th house

The lessons of forgiveness transform your life. By understanding past hurts, you'll access the power of acceptance. Since you can't change the past, you've chosen to heal the mind and emotions. This can lead to a new awareness and heightened consciousness.

Deep issues from the past led you to this understanding. Disturbing experiences brought sorrow, so now you're healing the past. By processing the pain, you've grown by leaps and bounds on a spiritual level, accumulating wisdom.

Like a sage, you're now approaching realization of the universal consciousness. You've been through many life experiences and come to the ultimate realization of life. You've surrendered your ego and now feel your oneness with God.

Ketu or Rahu in Aquarius or Capricorn: Saturn is dispositor

Saturn as the dispositor of Ketu or Rahu is more detached from the emotions of the world. Loss of love and feelings disconnect you from the world. A deep sense of responsibility overshadows life and the world.

Saturn gives back that which we have earned through discipline, perseverance, and hard work. Saturn is known to give us our greatest gifts through the attainment of wisdom.

With Ketu or Rahu in Capricorn or Aquarius, Saturn is the dispositor, and will therefore exert its influence through the houses as follows:

Saturn in the 1st house

You come into this world mature and wise. It's odd to be a baby because you're older than your years. With a deep sense of responsibility, you feel the need to care for others. It seems you never had the opportunity to be a child because you took on chores of an adult. Having cared for everyone else in previous lifetimes, you can't seem to escape this role.

In this life, give back responsibility to others by not enabling them. This is hard to do because it means you're breaking many lifetimes of the same pattern. Those you're helping may tend to cast guilt on you but that's all just part of this lifetime's growth.

Having been responsible for your past-life family of origin, the energy to care for your current family may be depleted. You shun this responsibility. It's time to set boundaries and move forward, seeking a new life with security built around your own family.

Saturn in the 2nd house

Early childhood had an array of family problems with a lack of security. Times were hard and parents gave mixed messages, typically around the lack or importance of money.

You were deprived of security because of the cold and detached nature of your parents. Because you were ridiculed when you spoke your mind, you learned to keep your thoughts to yourself. Who you are and what you expressed was always invalidated. So now you believe that what you have to say isn't important. This set up a pattern of insecurity in which you're afraid to speak your mind.

You're here in this lifetime to overcome the patterns of the past. You need to realize that who you are, what you think, and what you have to say is both valid and important. This will create a new you, full of confidence and credibility.

Saturn in the 3rd house

The focus of this life is to develop your ability to express yourself and not be concerned with criticism from others. Early education seemed difficult, maybe due to difficulties in the home. Overwhelmed by family issues, you lost your way.

But now, with discipline, you'll regain your focus and pave the way for educational accomplishments.

Siblings or their lack is an issue. You feel estranged from them or never felt included in their activities. This hampered your sense of feeling connected in the world.

In this life you'll use your discipline to develop some form of expression, eg, writing, to connect to others. Through teaching and guidance, you can develop your talent. Use it to express yourself, thus alleviating isolation and aloneness.

Saturn in the 4th house

Security in the home demands a lifelong search for fulfillment. The need to feel connected, heart and soul, is a constant quest. In the past you felt unloved, therefore ended up with the impression you were unlovable. Despite your best efforts, you still haven't learned how to love yourself.

The problem is, you never seem to accept love, even when it's given, because you feel unlovable. This is your life lesson, to open your heart, love yourself and to accept love.

This negative pattern originated with your mother in the past but now it's time to break the pattern. Your mother's behavior made you believe you were unlovable, but in reality she was just projecting her own issues. Accept that this was not the truth, and not your issue. Open your heart to give and receive love, and you'll finally be free of this handicap.

Saturn in the 5th house

With a probing mind, you're always asking mankind's eternal question: *Why are we here?* Frustration erupts when you can find no easy answers. But the quest never really ends.

Children bring a lifetime of lessons in opening your heart. Your kids become your teachers for the most important – learning unconditional love. A karmic debt must be paid via your children but the rewards are beyond words. The open-hearted love they bring heals eons of past karma. They free your soul.

Creative talents are harnessed to guide others. You're here as an advisor to give guidance to others. Your clients appreciate your honesty, loyalty and virtue. Even in the guise of a business, you find opportunities to share important lessons.

Saturn in the 6th house

Your sense of responsibility is stellar! You'd never consider being tardy or not finishing a project on time. You're the loyal and hardworking employee that everyone needs. But at some point your work ethic must take on a bigger challenge, to start your own business. It's time your talents made you the success you've made others in the past.

Discipline in the area of health is always your concern. At times you're fanatical about your health and diet. You may need to focus on diet because of issues with your digestion. Your health was a major concern in previous lifetimes and you're here to reconcile this now.

An awareness of your health on all levels concerns you. With diligence, you'll free yourself of the abuse over many lifetimes, and become healthy in body, mind and spirit. Remember, it's not just what you eat or drink but also exercise that can heal the mind of excessive worry. Stress causes wear and tear on the body too. Your health is your responsibility in this life.

Saturn in the 7th house

The quest to have a loving and lasting relationship is your karma in this lifetime. In your previous lives, relationships were difficult, and you felt lonely and isolated from love and affection. This lifetime you're seeking a partner who is loving and loyal.

However, you often choose a partner for the wrong reasons, typically for security. Although being taken care of is important, essentially you're the best guarantor of your own security. You've now reversed roles, meaning you should be the provider. This may feel uncomfortable this time around, but it's an essential lesson for this life.

Once the right relationship is established, you need to make it work. Lessons of the heart are a blessing in disguise. You'll grow by learning how to recognize real love, not confusing it with material security.

Saturn in the 8th house

In a previous lifetime, control and manipulation were at the core of your being. Now you must unravel these dark issues that lurk as your shadow selves in this lifetime.

The major issue is to let go of needing to be in control. The more you attempt to be in control, the more out of control you become. Learn to surrender. The Divine force will help you resolve this past karma. By letting go, you'll come to realize your addictive patterns. Release brings transformation, which frees up karma, bestowing glimpses of enlightenment.

The process of letting go is similar to death. Freed of your emotional burdens, you have the potential to gain wisdom.

Saturn in the 9th house

Hypocrisy among family and teachers has created cynical attitudes and defiant disbelief regarding authority figures. Your exposure to those who don't walk the talk has aroused skepticism regarding religious or political laws. When you don't know what to believe, and can't find the truth, you feel lost.

Your father was unemotional and detached, and planted feelings of emptiness in your soul. You sought teachers for emotional guidance but they always disappointed you.

Your lesson in life is to trust your own inner guidance and create a loving spiritual relationship within. You are your own teacher, but you need to rekindle the presence of the Divine within. In previous lifetimes you felt betrayed by spiritual laws because there appeared to be no justice. But according to the laws of karma, everything happens for a reason and that there is inevitably justice of the Divine. The end results are for the highest good.

Saturn in the 10th house

Your career showcases your accomplishments and growing importance in this life. You need to feel a purpose. The sense of responsibility and commitment is a powerful component of your life's resolution.

Rising to the top of your profession and achieving a position of authority is important to you. In a previous life, you were held back and never given what you deserved. But now you're given the opportunity to accomplish goals that were never addressed.

You're meant to be your own boss because you can't take orders from others any longer. You need to be in control. Once you achieve this position, success will inevitably follow.

Saturn in the 11th house

As the eldest or wisest of your siblings, you were given an important position. The family put you in charge and depended on you. But because you feel you let them down in previous lifetimes, now you need to redeem yourself. As you grow in stature, you'll assume more of a leadership role in taking care of them.

Powerful people come into your life to provide guidance. More importantly, they'll put you in positions of responsibility that can bring achievement and wealth.

Your accomplishments and connections could put you in a position of political prominence. You're sought after for your guidance. But you like to operate alone, because too many people around you can complicate your mission.

Saturn in the 12th house

You are your own worst enemy. Through your own condemnation, you may be stuck in a predicament. But you have the power to change your life, by refusing to be a victim anymore.

In this life, charity work can mend your karma from past lives when you were stingy and withholding. Today's poverty consciousness is only due to limitations you imposed on yourself in previous lifetimes.

Being a victim of the past distances you from the gifts you possess. Poverty and suffering are not your tickets to heaven. They only hold you back from the joys of this life. Letting go of painful memories involving grief and sorrow will unleash possibilities you've never imagined before.

CHAPTER 8

World Events: Revelations of Eclipses by Sign and Nakshatra

Transiting Rahu and Ketu stay in a sign for 18 months. There are two eclipses a year, six months apart occurring in opposing signs. The eclipses generally occur within 12-18 degrees of the positions of Rahu and Ketu. The sign they are in will determine the results of those eclipses but there are other details that give the Rahu/Ketu transit very specific results, particularly at the time of the eclipses.

Here are the factors that influence the results according to their placements:

1) Sign and nakshatra placement of Rahu and Ketu (eclipses)

2) Planets conjunct and opposed Rahu and Ketu (eclipses)

3) Fixed stars conjunct Rahu and Ketu (eclipses)

Planets conjunct an eclipse will lend their indications and meanings through the events produced. Slower-moving planets influence eclipses because they are in the sign with the nodes for a longer period. Saturn and Jupiter influence the nodes, especially in financial matters. Saturn is treacherous and Jupiter can expand and magnify dangerous effects. The outer planets Uranus, Neptune, and Pluto can cause extremes according to their nature. Uranus indicates sudden unexpected events, Neptune indicates deception and delusions, and Pluto brings power struggles. Mars is a trigger when it aspects Rahu and Ketu, activating events at the time of aspect, generally provoking violence.

The signs of Rahu and Ketu will flavor the experience according to their nature and meanings. The nakshatras give specific meanings, typically in accordance with the meaning of fixed stars in this portion of the zodiac. If an eclipse is conjunct a fixed star it will give the results of that star.

Table 1: Zodiacal placements of Nakshatras

Nakshatras		Zodiacal Position	Ruling Planets	Planetary Periods in Years
1) *Ashwini*	"the horse woman"	00.00 ♈ to 13.20 ♈	Ketu	7
2) *Bharani*	"the bearer - of new life"	13.20 ♈ to 26.40 ♈	Venus	20
3) *Krittika*	"the one who cuts"	26.40 ♈ to 10.00 ♉	Sun	6
4) *Rohini*	"the red one"	10.00 ♉ to 23.20 ♉	Moon	10
5) *Mrigashira*	"head of a deer"	23.20 ♉ to 06.40 ♊	Mars	7
6) *Ardra*	"the moist one"	06.40 ♊ to 20.00 ♊	Rahu	18
7) *Punarvasu*	"return of the light"	20.00 ♊ to 03.20 ♋	Jupiter	16
8) *Pushya*	"to nourish"	03.20 ♋ to 16.40 ♋	Saturn	19
9) *Ashlesha*	"the embracer"	16.40 ♋ to 30.00 ♋	Mercury	17
10) *Magha*	"the great one"	00.00 ♌ to 13.20 ♌	Ketu	7
11) *Purva Phalguni*	"the former reddish one"	13.20 ♌ to 26.40 ♌	Venus	20
12) *Uttara Phalguni*	"the later reddish one"	26.40 ♌ to 10.00 ♍	Sun	6
13) *Hasta*	"the hand"	10.00 ♍ to 23.20 ♍	Moon	10
14) *Chitra*	"the bright one"	23.20 ♍ to 06.40 ♎	Mars	7
15) *Swati*	"the sword" or "independence"	06.40 ♎ to 20.00 ♎	Rahu	18
16) *Vishaka*	"the forked shaped"	20.00 ♎ to 03.20 ♏	Jupiter	16
17) *Anurada*	"the disciple of the divine spark"	03.20 ♏ to 16.40 ♏	Saturn	19
18) *Jyeshta*	"the eldest"	16.40 ♏ to 00.00 ♐	Mercury	17
19) *Mula*	"the root"	00.00 ♐ to 13.20 ♐	Ketu	7
20) *Purva Ashadha*	"early victory"	13.20 ♐ to 26.40 ♐	Venus	20
21) *Uttara Ashadha*	"Latter victory"	26.40 ♐ to 10.00 ♑	Sun	6
22) *Shravana*	"to hear"	10.00 ♑ to 23.20 ♑	Moon	10
23) *Dhanishta*	"the richest one"	23.20 ♑ to 06.40 ♒	Mars	7
24) *Shatabhishak*	"a hundred healers"	06.40 ♒ to 20.00 ♒	Rahu	18
25) *Purva Bhadrapada*	"the former happy feet"	20.00 ♒ to 03.20 ♓	Jupiter	16
26) *Uttara Bhadrapada*	"the latter happy feet"	03.20 ♓ to 16.40 ♓	Saturn	19
27) *Revati*	"the wealthy"	16.40 ♓ to 30.00 ♓	Mercury	17

Table 2: Fixed Stars

Fixed Stars

Fixed Star	Description	Western Position	Vedic Position
El Sheratan	"the two signs ". This star represents danger when acting impulsively	3.58 Taurus	10.07 Aries
Almach	cheerful nature, likes change and variety. Popularity brings benefit from others	14.14 Taurus	20.63 Aries
Menkar	associated with disgrace and loss of fortune	14.19 Taurus	20.68 Aries
Alcyone - The Weeping Sisters	brightest, star of sorrow and also star of success and prominence	0.00 Gemini	6.49 Taurus
Algol - The Weeping Sisters	demon, most violent and evil of stars. Deals with losing one 's head, figuratively and literally	26.10 Taurus	2.59 Taurus
Aldebaran -The Weeping Sisters	honor, intelligence, extraordinary energy and enthusiasm, but threat of danger from enemies	9.47 Gemini	15.96 Taurus
Betelgeuse	martial honor, power, and wealth	28.45 Gemini	4.94 Gemini
Sirius	considered royal one, but also quite violent, gives honor beyond grave, famous death	14.05 Cancer	20.54 Gemini
Castor - Gemini Twin	the mortal twin, known or his sharp intellect, fame and honor with loss of fortune	20.14 Cancer	26.63 Gemini
Pollux - Gemini Twin	immortal twin, known for fighting skills, known for courage and ruthlessness	23.13 Cancer	29.62 Gemini
Acubens	nurturing and preserving, but nervous nature. Good for affairs with public	13.39 Leo	19.88 Cancer
Regulus	royal fixed star noted for kings and leaders, great fame, and quest for power	29.50 Leo	5.99 Leo

Algenubi (shows as Denebola)	gives creative, artistic abilities	21.37 Virgo	27.86 Leo
Zosma	star of egotism and self-indulgence	11.19 Virgo	17.68 Leo
Algorab	star of hindrances, success in business but eventual falls	13.27 Libra	19.76 Virgo
Spica	one of the most auspicious stars of all denoting success, fame, honors, wealth, and a love of the arts and sciences	23.50 LIbra	29.99 Virgo
Acturus	gives riches, renown prosperity and success in fine arts	24.14 Libra	0.63 Libra
Antares	high intelligence, honors and power, but with sudden loss. Political and Military star	9.46 Libra	15.95 Scorpio
Kaus Borealis	associated with idealistic, altruistic qualities, and a strong need for justice	6.19 Capricorn	12.68 Sagittarius
Galactic Center	where cosmic intelligence originates. Center of the galaxy	26 Sagittarius	2.49 Sagittarius
Altair	gives a bold, bright, ambitious nature. It leads to positions of power, but trouble with authority	1.47 Aquarius	7.96 Capricorn
Fomalhaut	can be very treacherous or very benefic. Possesses creativity, especially musical talent	3.52 Pisces	10.01 Aquarius
Markab	headstrong nature. Fated star of sorrow	23.28 Pisces	29.77 Aquarius
Sheat	star of literary and poetic ability, but also implies extreme loss and sorrow	29.22 Pisces	5.71 Pisces

Rahu and Ketu in Aries (Ashwini, Bharani, Krittika) and Libra (Chitra, Swati, Vishaka)

The cardinal signs Aries and Libra are powerful action-oriented signs that produce big events. The fire and air elements of Aries and Libra are instigators that constitute new beginnings. Progressive thinking and problem solving are the end result of events that transpire

100

while Rahu and Ketu create eclipses here. Some events can be dangerous with the level of brash and impulsive energy that comes with this territory.

The nakshatra Bharani can instigate great obstacles to overcome and, through persistence, brings breakthroughs and breakdowns in global affairs. The 1929 stock market crash occurred while Rahu was in Aries and Ketu in Libra. This was the beginning of the Great Depression.

Rahu was in Aries and Ketu in Libra when a devastating tsunami hit Malaysia at the very end of 2004. The Indian Ocean earthquake occurred on December 26, 2004, with the epicenter off the west coast of Sumatra, Indonesia. The shock had a magnitude of 9.1–9.3. An estimated 280,000 people died. This quake affected many countries.

The nakshatra Swati is ruled by Rahu and can have devastating effects. The nakshatra Ashwini is ruled by Ketu, compounding the effects of Rahu and Ketu. The stock market crash had Ketu in Swati. The tsunami of Malaysia had Rahu in Ashwini.

2nd h.	3rd h.	4th h.	5th h.
♅℞ 16:34 UBh	☊ 19:39 Bha	♃ 23:30 Mrg	♀ 26:40 Pun
1st h. ASC 11:43 Sat	Stock Market Crash Tue 10-01-1929 16:15:43 New York, New York USA Timezone: 5 DST: 0 Latitude: 40N42'51 Longitude: 74W00'22 Ayanamsha : -22:52:21 Lahiri		6th h.
12th h.		♆ 09:35 Mag ♀ 14:39 PPh	7th h.
♄ 01:56 Mul	♂ 03:59 Cht ☋ 19:39 Swa		☽ 01:59 UPh ☉ 15:19 Has ☿℞ 28:13 Cht
11th h.	10th h.	9th h.	8th h.

Rahu and Ketu

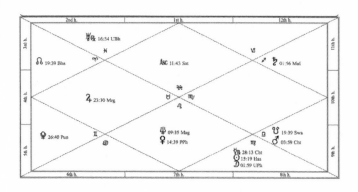

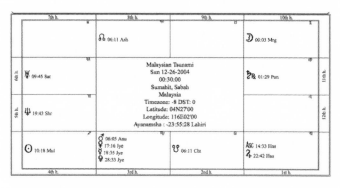

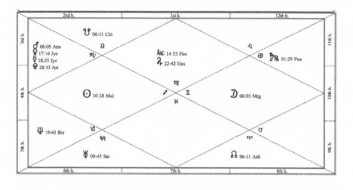

Rahu and Ketu in Taurus (Krittika, Rohini, Mrigashira) and Scorpio (Vishaka, Anuradha, Jyeshta)

In the fixed signs of Taurus and Scorpio, things seem to consolidate and deepen. This may be the time that discoveries and revelations surface.

On a positive note, Alexander Fleming discovered penicillin in 1928 while Ketu was in Scorpio (with Saturn). This saved many lives and was a huge medical breakthrough for the world. It seems the nodes in Taurus/Scorpio can give good results. This could be due to the exaltation of the nodes in these signs. Rahu exalted in Taurus and Ketu exalted in Scorpio.

This is the time that Japan reorganized their country after World War 2 and made a remarkable industrial comeback after such widespread destruction.

It seems this portion of the zodiac facilitates the revelation of discoveries to make the world a better place − positive and healing results after deep turmoil and devastation.

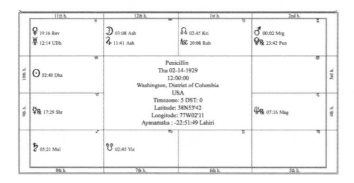

Rahu and Ketu

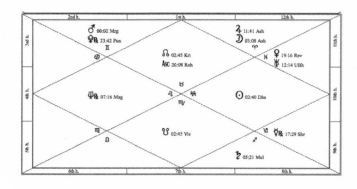

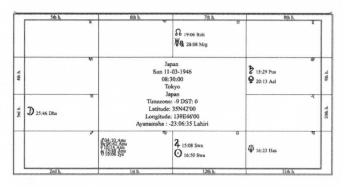

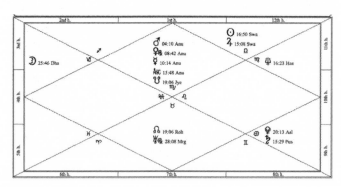

Rahu and Ketu in Gemini (Mrigashira, Ardra, Punarvasu) and Sagittarius (Mula, Purva Ashadha, Uttara Ashadha)

This is the most treacherous portion of the zodiac for Rahu and Ketu.

While Rahu was in Gemini in the nakshatra Ardra, the most horrific events occurred – the bombing of Hiroshima in 1945, the assassination of President John F. Kennedy in 1963, and the 9/11 attacks on America in 2001. For all these dates, Rahu was in Gemini in the nakshatra Ardra. Saturn was conjunct Rahu for the Hiroshima bomb. On 9/11 Jupiter was conjunct Rahu, and Mars was conjunct Ketu.

These horrific events are associated with the birth chart of the US where four powerful planets (Mars, Venus, Sun and Jupiter) occupy the sign of Gemini. Obviously, there appears to be a connection between events and the charts of the countries where these events are likely to occur.

Ardra is ruled by the storm god Rudra symbolized by the howling wind and the tear drop. It is the nakshatra of tragic events. Gemini as an air sign indicates messages or tragedy through the air or transportation. Bombs were dropped by aircraft on Hiroshima. Airplanes were used as weapons of mass destruction in 9/11. Kennedy was traveling in a vehicle when he was shot.

Ketu in Sagittarius is a difficult place, particularly in the nakshatra Mula. This nakshatra indicates destruction because Niritti the goddess of destruction rules over Mula. Furthermore, this is the point of the Galactic Center where astronomers have detected the largest concentration of black holes in the Universe. Black holes are known to be like a vacuum and could be the entry to other dimensions.

The area following Mula in Sagittarius is Purva Ashadha which is known for declarations of war. Many times the nodes passing through this portion of the zodiac brings war.

As horrific as these events have been in history, the signs and nakshatras are part of an evolution that eventually brings opportunities for healing. Destruction clears the path for rebuilding. The nakshatra following Ardra is Punarvasu, which means the return of the light. Even after the darkest storms comes a sunny day.

As the nodes transit through Gemini and Sagittarius, the truth that is revealed comes through our worst nightmares − violence, death, sorrow. It is the release of the buildup from mounting pressure. Just as deep emotion produces tears, so too do storm clouds accumulate moisture till they burst with rain. What comes out of the dark, or is revealed at that time, are issues surrounding suffering and pain. What comes out of tragedy is the unity of people to heal the suffering and pain of isolation.

The fixed star Betelgeuse around 4-5 degrees of Gemini is known to produce assassinations, explosions and lightning.

The Great Chicago Fire burned from Sunday to early Tuesday, October 8-10, 1871. The fire killed up to 300 people, destroyed roughly 3.3 square miles of Chicago, and left more than 100,000 residents homeless. Saturn was conjunct Ketu in Mula.

The AIDS epidemic killed more people than any disease over time. The first AIDS case recognized in the US was in 1982, with Rahu in Gemini, Ketu in Sagittarius.

Rahu and Ketu

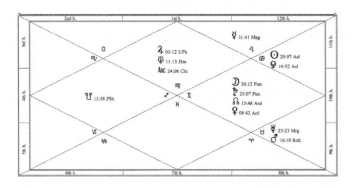

7th h.	8th h.	9th h.	10th h.
		♂ 16:10 Roh ♅ 23:23 Mrg	♀ 08:42 Ard ☊ 15:48 Ard ♄ 25:07 Pun ☽ 26:12 Pun
6th h.	Hiroshima Attack Mon 08-06-1945 10:35:23 Hiroshima Japan Timezone: -9 DST: 0 Latitude: 34N23'00 Longitude: 132E28'00 Ayanamsha : -23:05:34 Lahiri		♆ 16:52 Asl ☉ 20:07 Asl **11th h.**
5th h.			☿ 11:41 Mag **12th h.**
☋ 15:48 PSh			♃ 03:12 UPh ♆ 11:15 Has ASC 24:08 Cht
4th h.	3rd h.	2nd h.	1st h.

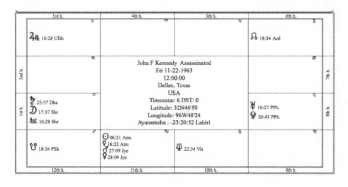

John F Kennedy Assassinated
Fri 11-22-1963
12:00:00
Dallas, Texas
USA
Timezone: 6 DST: 0
Latitude: 32N46'59
Longitude: 96W48'24
Ayanamsha : -23:20:52 Lahiri

3rd h.	4th h.	5th h.	6th h.
♃℞ 16:28 UBh			☊ 18:34 Ard
2nd h.			**7th h.**
♄ 23:57 Dha ☽ 17:37 Shr ASC 16:28 Shr			♅ 16:27 PPh **8th h.** ♀ 20:43 PPh
☋ 18:34 PSh	☉ 06:21 Anu ♆ 16:22 Anu ♂ 27:09 Jye ☿ 28:04 Jye	♃ 22:34 Vis	
12th h.	11th h.	10th h.	9th h.

107

Rahu and Ketu

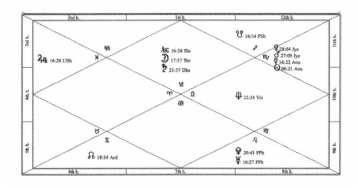

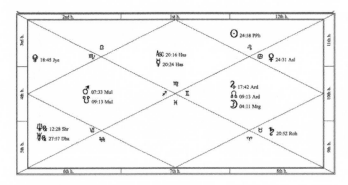

108

Rahu and Ketu

USA
Thu 07-04-1776
18:30:00
Philadelphia, Pennsylvania
USA
Timezone: 5 DST: 0
Latitude: 39N57'08
Longitude: 75W09'51
Ayanamsha: -20:43:59 Lahiri

⛢ 18:12 Roh
♂ 00:41 Mrg
☊ 12:27 Ard
♃ 15:13 Ard
☉ 22:39 Pun
☽ 07:14 Sat
♀ 03:26 Pus
☋ 16:51 Asl
☊ 16:51 Shr
♀℞ 10:44 Shr
ASC 08:50 Mul
♆ 01:41 UPh
♄ 24.04 Cht

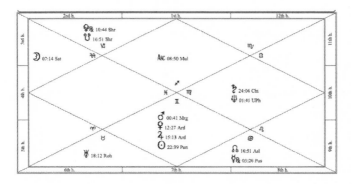

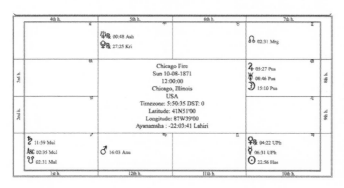

Chicago Fire
Sun 10-08-1871
12:00:00
Chicago, Illinois
USA
Timezone: 5:50:35 DST: 0
Latitude: 41N51'00
Longitude: 87W39'00
Ayanamsha: -22:03:41 Lahiri

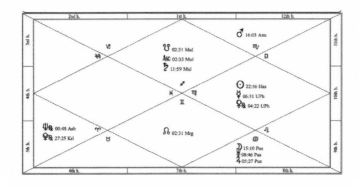

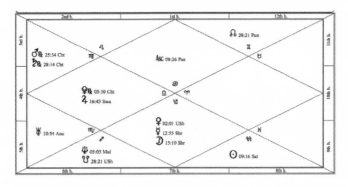

Rahu and Ketu in Cancer (Punarvasu, Pushya, Ashlesha) and Capricorn (Uttara Ashadha, Shravana, Dhanishta)

The placement of Rahu and Ketu in Cancer and Capricorn can affect the security of a nation. The most destructive earthquake to ever hit California destroyed the city of San Francisco in 1906, when Rahu was in Cancer and Ketu in Capricorn.

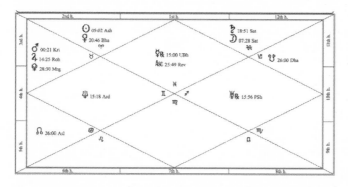

Rahu and Ketu in Leo (Magha, Purva Phalguni, Uttara Phalguni) and Aquarius (Dhanishta, Shatabhishak, Purva Bhadrapada)

The Japanese surprise attack on Pearl Harbor, December 7, 1941, precipitated the entry of the United States into World War 2. Since Leo indicates leadership, control and taking charge, the presence of Rahu in Leo, Ketu in Aquarius, can indicate fighting back, or the emergence of events pertaining to controversy or war.

During the 2016 U.S. Presidential elections, the media induced the election results. This was due to the eclipses falling in Leo and Aquarius, involving Neptune's deception, deceit and dishonesty, which could have been said about every politician in the world at this time. There's corruption in Turkey, South and North Korea, Malaysia, Brazil, China, France and the U.S., to name just a few. An attempted coup in Turkey took the country by surprise in July 2016 but the government turned it to their favor.

Rahu is in Leo, Ketu in Aquarius with Neptune, from January 2016 to September 2017.

In 1997-1998 there was a scandal involving Monica Lewinsky and President Clinton. President Clinton was impeached and charged with perjury but was acquitted of the charges. Rahu was in Leo, Ketu in Aquarius. Scandalous affairs seem to surface when the nodes are transiting these signs. Jupiter was conjunct Ketu in Shatabhishak.

The eclipses in Leo and Aquarius revealed truth but many chose not to see it. There is a great effort to cover up facts. But the truth will surface as it did with the Clintons both times, 1998 and 2016.

The death of Princess Diana occurred August 31, 1997, when Rahu was in Leo and Ketu in Aquarius. Many conspiracy theorists believe this was no accident.

♂ 22:33 Rev

♄℞ 00:26 Kri
♅℞ 04:35 Kri
♃℞ 23:26 Mrg

☽ 07:21 Pus
♀℞ 12:31 Pus

☋ 24:58 PBh
ASC 18:39 Sat

♀ 08:43 USh

☊ 24:58 PPh

Pearl Harbor
Sun 12-07-1941
12:00:00
Honolulu, Hawaii
USA
Timezone: 10:30:00 DST: 0
Latitude: 21N18'25
Longitude: 157W51'30
Ayanamsa : -23:02:41 Lahiri

☿ 14:37 Anu
☉ 22:24 Jye

♆ 06:39 UPh

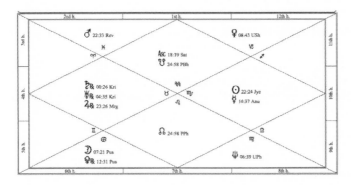

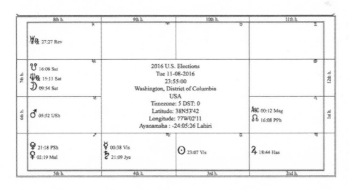

113

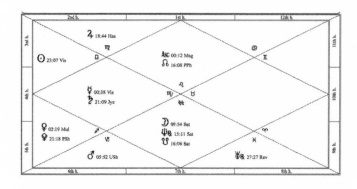

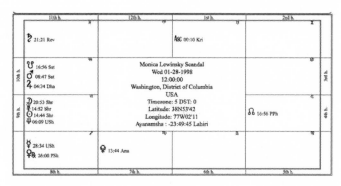

Monica Lewinsky Scandal
Wed 01-28-1998
12:00:00
Washington, District of Columbia
USA
Timezone: 5 DST: 0
Latitude: 38N53'42
Longitude: 77W02'11
Ayanamsha : -23:49:45 Lahiri

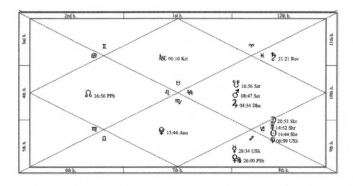

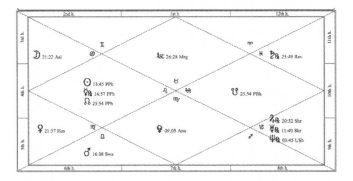

Rahu and Ketu in Virgo (Uttara Phalguni, Hasta, Chitra) and Pisces (Purva Bhadrapada, Uttara Bhadrapada)

During the Paris attacks November 13, 2015, at least 128 were killed in gunfire and blasts during a concert in the Bataclan night club. Rahu was in Virgo with Mars. This alerted the world to the terror taking place all over Europe, and the specter of more to come. Interestingly enough, the birth charts of the countries under attack are connected. In the chart for France, Rahu is in Virgo and Ketu is in Pisces.

Rahu and Ketu

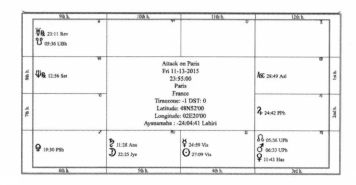

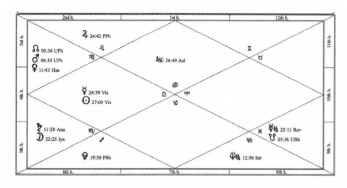

116

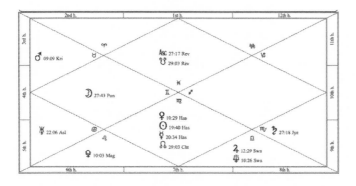

Rahu and Ketu in Libra (Chitra, Swati, Vishaka) and Aries (Ashwini, Bharani, Krittika)

Malaysian flight MH370 disappeared without a trace into the Indian Ocean. To this day no one knows for sure what happened. Rahu was in Libra (conjunct Saturn and Mars) and Ketu was in Aries. Rahu in air signs often indicates problems with air travel.

The weather seems to be better cold when Saturn is conjunct Rahu.

Columbus discovered America in 1492 when Rahu was in Libra and Ketu in Aries. With Ketu in the sign of pioneers and new discoveries, America was finally discovered by the Europeans.

President Lincoln was assassinated April 14, 1865, when Saturn and Rahu were in Libra.

World War 2 started September 1, 1939, while Rahu was in Libra (Swati) and Ketu was in Aries (Ashwini). This was the beginning of one of the most violent and disastrous periods in history.

What surfaces during eclipses in these signs is the seething anger that causes the world to explode with violence.

When Rahu is in an air sign there's often very bad weather and earth changes.

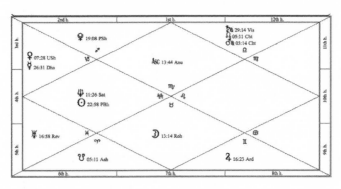

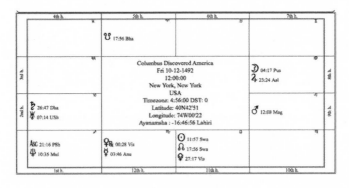

118

Rahu and Ketu

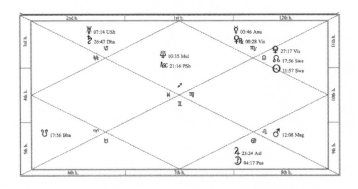

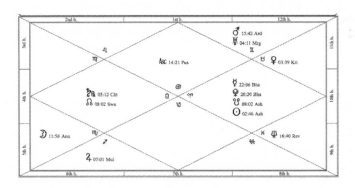

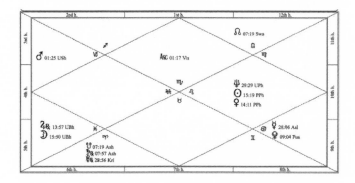

Rahu and Ketu in Scorpio (Vishaka, Anurada, Jyeshta) and Taurus (Krittika, Rohini, Mrigashira)

Rahu was in Scorpio and Ketu in Taurus on September 8, 1900. This was one of the deadliest events in US history where 6,000-12,000 died in Galveston, Texas, due to the worse hurricane to ever hit the U.S.

Jupiter was tightly conjunct Rahu with Uranus in Scorpio, and Pluto with Ketu. Jupiter will magnify the result of Uranus, which is often involved in unexpected tragic events. During that era, storms of this magnitude were not foreseen by contemporary weather forecasting technology.

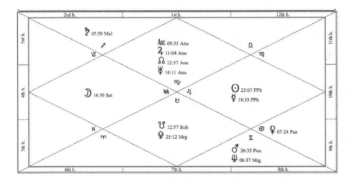

Rahu and Ketu in Sagittarius (Mula, Purva Ashadha, Uttara Ashadha) and Gemini (Mrigashira, Ardra, Punarvasu)

This is the flip side of a treacherous placement for Rahu and Ketu, because here we have Ketu in Gemini in tragic Ardra and Rahu in the destructive nakshatra Mula. One of the most destructive earthquakes in history was in Japan on March 11, 2011. Rahu was in Mula at 4 degrees Sagittarius conjunct the Galactic Center. What seems to come out of such tragedy is the clearing-away for the new, but it still causes much human suffering.

The 9.1-magnitude earthquake northeast of Tokyo, the largest to hit Japan, caused a tsunami with 30-foot waves that damaged several nuclear reactors in the area. The combined total of confirmed deaths and missing was more than 22,000.

In the 1918 pandemic that killed over 50 million people, Rahu was in Sagittarius and Ketu in Gemini. Here again, this treacherous portion of the zodiac is vulnerable to transits of Rahu and Ketu that can spell tragedy for many.

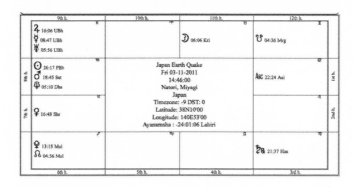

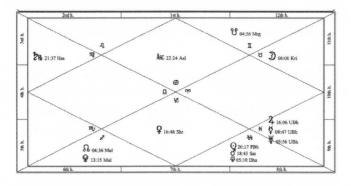

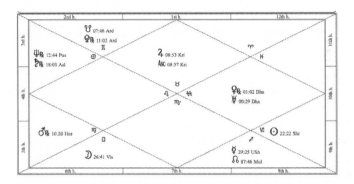

Rahu and Ketu in Capricorn (Uttara Ashadha, Shravana, Dhanishta) and Cancer (Punarvasu, Pushya, Ashlesha)

The Berlin Wall came down November 9, 1989, when Rahu was at 28 degrees Capricorn, and Ketu was in Cancer. This was a day of healing and reunification for homeland Germany, and a new era for Europe if not the world.

The stock market crash in 2008 had a devastating effect on the U.S economy. This event threatened the financial security of the U.S. because the country's birth chart for the U.S. has these very placements in the 8th

house of trauma. Rahu was in Capricorn conjunct
Neptune, but no one saw this one coming. Neptune with
Rahu indicates deception and corruption. Many got away
with millions in profits, with no consequences. Enormous
scandals were rampant during this time.

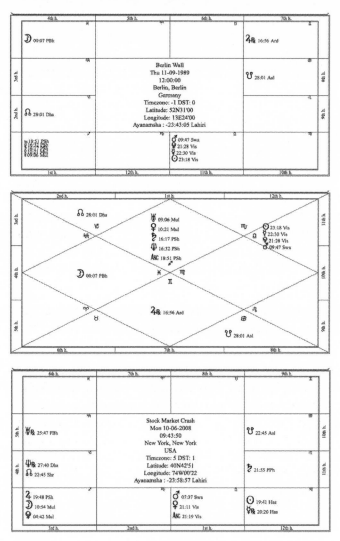

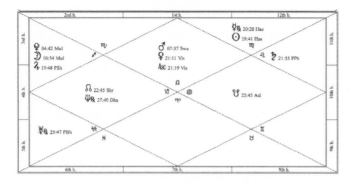

Rahu and Ketu in Aquarius (Dhanishta, Shatabhishak, Purva Bhadrapada) and Leo (Magha, Purva Phalguni, Uttara Phalguni)

The Tiananmen Square Massacre of 1989 occurred with Rahu in Aquarius and Ketu in Leo. The student-led demonstrations in Beijing were forcibly suppressed after the government declared martial law, and troops with assault rifles and tanks killed thousands of demonstrators trying to block the military's advance into the square.

Rahu and Ketu in the signs of Aquarius and Leo frequently point to governments in opposition to their own people or humanity.

The Pan Am airline crash over Lockerbie, Scotland, on December 21, 1988, was an early terrorist attack. Rahu was in Aquarius in nakshatra Shatabhishak is ruled by Rahu. It appears that when Rahu transits nakshatras ruled by Rahu, the results can be treacherous especially for air travel. Rahu-ruled nakshatras (Ardra, Swati and Shatabhishak) are in air signs Gemini, Libra and Aquarius.

Rahu and Ketu

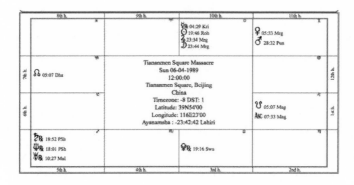

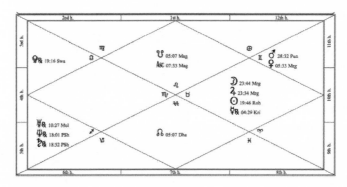

126

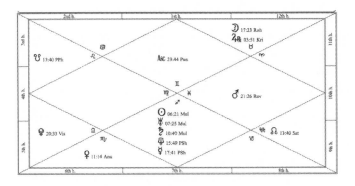

Rahu and Ketu in Pisces (Purva Bhadrapada, Uttara Bhadrapada, Revati) and Virgo (Uttara Phalguni, Hasta, Chitra)

Rahu was in Pisces, Ketu in Virgo, in 1968 when Martin Luther King Jr and Robert (Bobby) Kennedy were assassinated. Also during this time was the largest loss of life of American soldiers in the Vietnam War. With corruption at its peak in many governments, this was the time of rebellion, and youth around the world were fighting back.

Saturn was with Rahu during the King and Kennedy assassinations, with devastating results for the civil rights movement. When Saturn and Rahu conjoin by transit, there seems to be overwhelming and sad events. Saturn was with Rahu (in Libra) when President Lincoln was assassinated, and together in Gemini when the atomic bomb was dropped on Hiroshima.

Rahu was in the last degrees of Pisces when the Titanic sank April 15th, 1912. The last degrees of a water sign are *ghandanta* which means drowning. Over 1500 people lost their lives in this tragedy.

127

Hurricane Katrina hit New Orleans on August 29, 2005. Ketu was tightly conjoined Jupiter in Virgo. When Rahu is in Pisces, it seems the waters rise and cause destruction, while Jupiter's involvement magnifies the potential.

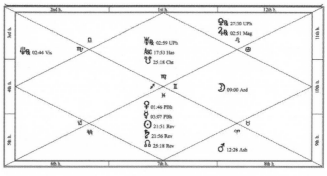

Rahu and Ketu

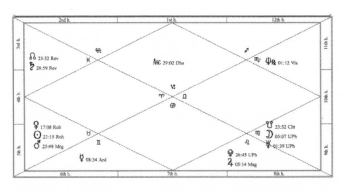

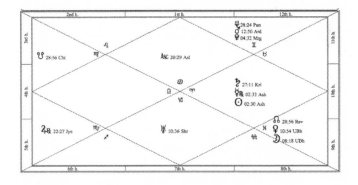

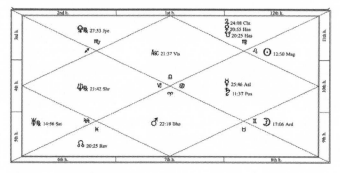

Future Predictions

Based on the analysis of history, the years of 2019-2020 look like a dangerous time. Rahu will be in Gemini, Ketu in Sagittarius. In May 2019, Rahu will be with Mars, and Ketu with Saturn.

By the end of 2019 Saturn and Jupiter will conjoin Ketu in Mula while Rahu occupies the nakshatra Ardra. In January 2020 Saturn will conjoin Pluto and Jupiter while Ketu is in Mula, and Rahu is in Ardra. This will produce an event that will shake the world. By the end of January 2020, Saturn will transit into Capricorn while Mars is in Scorpio. They will thus flank Jupiter and Ketu (in Sagittarius), placing them in a combination known as *papa kartari*, ie, flanked on either side by malefics.

Jupiter and Ketu in nakshatras Purva Ashadha and Uttara Ashadha may herald war because this is the nakshatra for the beginning of war.

From February 8 to March 23, 2020, Mars will be in Sagittarius with Jupiter. On February 25, Mars will conjoin Ketu in Mula while Rahu is in Ardra. This could be a time for catastrophic events, since Jupiter magnifies the circumstances. During this time, transiting Saturn and Pluto will be together in Capricorn. This suggests the breakdown of corruption in governments.

There's a solar eclipse on December 26, 2019, at 10 degrees Sagittarius. Transiting Mars will cross this degree on February 21-23, 2020. Mars will be in Mula, just two (2) degrees from Ketu and in the same sign with Jupiter, while Rahu is in Ardra. This is very similar to the aspects that were operating at the time of 9/11. The difference is that Jupiter was conjunct Rahu, but this time is with Ketu.

On 9/11, transiting Mars crossed by exact opposition to the previous solar eclipse degree. This was a critical time astrologically in the history of our world. Events are building currently to this time of tragedy (Ardra) and destruction (Mula). With conscious awareness this event could be averted. But at the time of this writing in 2017, the awareness on planet Earth is very low.

7th h.		8th h.		9th h.		10th h.	
		℞ 08:37 Ash				☊ 14:15 Ard	
6th h.	♆ 22:01 PBh		Solar Eclipse 2019 Thu 12-26-2019 00:14:00 Washington, District of Columbia USA				11th h.
5th h.	♀ 13:10 Shr		Timezone: 5 DST: 0 Latitude: 38N53'42 Longitude: 77W02'11 Ayanamsha : -24:07:54 Lahiri				12th h.
		♂ 00:22 Vis				ASC 10:37 Has	
4th h.		3rd h.		2nd h.		1st h.	

131

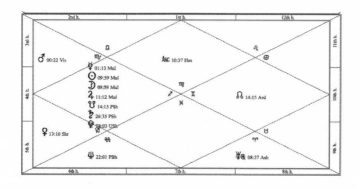

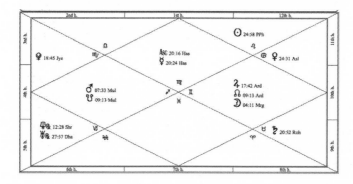

CHAPTER 9

Rahu and Ketu Transiting the 12 Houses

How Rahu and Ketu affect us on a personal level

Rahu and Ketu highlight the areas of life most likely to experience change via the houses they transit. Remember, wherever Rahu and Ketu are transiting, that is where the eclipses will occur that year. Since eclipses represent shadows, there's always something to be revealed, or some unknown upon which light may be shed, thus illuminating a problem or identifying what needs to be healed. When Rahu and Ketu change signs every 18 months, we have a fresh opportunity to peer into unknown areas of our life to identify what needs healing. It may not be easy, but is necessary for our growth and enlightenment.

If we look back 18.6 years, we can see where previous eclipses occurred in our chart, and perhaps realize that the issue concerning that house will recur, potentially unlocking our spiritual potential. Eclipse cycles in one's life have the potential, via the secrets they unlock, to bring our deeper karmic issues to the surface.

The houses Rahu and Ketu transit in your chart provide an indication of the lessons for the next 18 months.

Rahu transits the 1st; Ketu transits the 7th

Rahu in the 1st house can affect personal relationships due to Ketu's opposition transiting the 7th house. Relationships will be tested and anything repressed will almost certainly surface. If the relationship isn't on good terms, this will likely cause a breakup, but most solid relationships will go through a testing period that will strengthen the bond through growth together. There may be an old love or someone surface from the past to inspire love and romance.

Life may take on a fated quality as events develop and take an entirely different direction than previously planned. Life can change dramatically if the Universal forces have a different plan. Embrace the changes because they're directing life in a positive new direction.

Losses for the partner may involve major health problems that need medical attention. Career problems and personal losses of any kind can damage the partner's self-confidence and diminish self-esteem to the level of depression. Don't ignore these issues because they can be serious.

Eclipses occurring in these opposite houses suggest you should examine those aspects of yourself that are revealed through relationships. Something may be revealed regarding insecurity in relationships, perhaps a fear of being alone, or high expectations of your partner. It is time to heal your relationships.

Rahu transits the 2nd; Ketu transits the 8th

Rahu transiting the 2nd house pertains to money and finances. This can be a time of gains and losses depending on how money is handled. The financial situation may involve marriage, divorce or inheritance. Whatever the predicament, financially there'll be extremes of gains or losses.

There'll be a dramatic shift with an unexpected opportunity. Expect the unexpected with money. It isn't wise to gamble or take risks.

The consumption of food or drink may be excessive, revealing addictive behaviors. Problems with eyesight or teeth may require immediate attention, and costly dental work.

Deep psychological work can promote healing of the emotional body and a release from the controlling past. Psychic development opens the mind to new ideas and studies. Communication with spirits and otherworldly beings comes naturally. Interest in new metaphysical studies may emerge.

Eclipses falling in these opposite houses indicate anxiety or fear concerning money. Issues from the past, or past lives, surface now regarding insecurities around money. Unconscious and addictive behaviors that surface at this time need to be addressed and healed.

Rahu transits the 3rd; Ketu transits the 9th

Rahu in the 3rd house will promote travel. Opportunities to fly off to new places will satisfy the curious mind. Acquiring more connections will promote business in the future. Willpower, drive and a competitive spirit inspire you to improve your life's position.

There's a definite change in your attitude and involvement with new people. New business contracts are signed, promoting a new level of opportunity. Business will come from mass communications, eg, the internet, television, or radio. Be open to new ways for transferring information.

Problems and upsets with siblings may be a major concern. The father is on a steady decline and his health should be monitored. He may have retired from work, or is preparing for a big change. He may be depressed over a recent loss.

The need to explore spiritual growth inspires travel to mystical places. Unethical teachers or cult leaders may spoil the spiritual quest, but the understanding that a teacher is unnecessary breeds new vision and potential enlightenment.

New beliefs change your life direction and bring a deep awareness of changing consciousness. Through an understanding of the divine laws of the Universe, past events can now bring clarity to the future.

This is not the time to pursue legal actions, or to contend with immigration legalities.

Eclipses falling in these opposite houses suggest fears from the past concerning deep seated beliefs and how you relate to others. There's a disconnection, and a loss of meaning or purpose in life. The truth of who you are is emerging so that you can appreciate the meaning of your life and how it relates to others.

Rahu transits the 4th; Ketu transits the 10th

Rahu in the 4th house manifests many changes in home life. People will move in and out of the home. It may be time to buy or sell a house, with a related change of lifestyle.

Unexpected career shifts can give rise to great success, but an adaptable attitude is necessary. This career move will have a major effect on your surroundings, requiring a major move. This could mean many changes in home life. The career can determine where to live during this time.

Life is transforming dramatically. Be careful not to overextend yourself with house payments or unnecessary new items. There's pressure to change the direction of your life, and move both residence and office. Be patient and don't make dramatic changes during this time because they won't last.

The mother may experience new opportunities that promote her independence. Car problems may indicate it's time to buy a new car.

Eclipses falling in these opposite houses indicate issues concerning family matters and a need to find security. Fears around separation and lack of love and connection to family emerge due to past loneliness.

Rahu transits the 5th; Ketu transits the 11th

Rahu in the 5th house can cause obsessive and compulsive behavior. This is a time for mulling over ideas and plans. Past memories may emerge concerning regrets about the past.

There may be great achievements and advancements for children. Changes in the home may mean a new birth or the beginning of an empty-nest scenario. Extraordinary ideas come in flashes of inspiration, but think twice, because there's a fine line between genius and insanity.

Intrigue with new ideas can transform your life. An involvement in investments and speculation can deliver major windfalls.

Love of the arts and entertainment bring happy outings and fun. Sporting events bring some needed relief, plus renewed connections with old friends.

Unusual or unconventional friends may disturb your better judgment. Don't be persuaded by any unscrupulous ideas, because if it appears too good to be true, then it is.

This is a good time to socialize in the political arena, paying attention to humanitarian causes and charities for the betterment of humanity.

Eclipses falling in these opposite houses suggest that you're remembering your purpose in terms of how you express yourself. You can't be fulfilled unless you can see what you've created. Your purpose in life becomes clear as your accomplishments are manifested. Friends may be important in helping you see this truth.

Rahu transits the 6th; Ketu transits the 12th

Rahu in the 6th house can cause stress to the physical body. Ketu in the 12th may even prompt a visit to the hospital. A potential health scare can motivate a change in your habits, which will promote better health in the future. This is an opportunity to change bad habits.

Co-workers or employees can't be trusted or depended upon. Employees seem to quit at the most stressful times. This is not a good time to hire any new employees, because there could be someone disreputable among them.

Co-workers may steal ideas or clients, so don't reveal sensitive information. Gossip behind the scenes may cause problems at work, and sleepless nights through worry.

In a similar vein, take the appropriate precautions with security systems and alarms. Enemies of one kind or another may surface at this time, so be aware of anyone lurking around the home or workplace.

People may appear from the past, causing you to relive old memories. Legal disputes may also emerge, but if you have the strength to persevere in the face of the odds, you can still win a case.

Eclipses falling in these opposite houses suggest a message about how you take care of yourself and others. Your health is a source of major concern, even anxiety. On the plus side, however, a fear of disease is a sign that it's time to take care of your health. Although your bias is to think of others, focus on caring for yourself.

Rahu transits the 7th; Ketu transits the 1st

Rahu in the 7th house can attract a new relationship. The partner becomes more demanding and it difficult to make peace. Extreme behavior may escalate that can break many marriages during this intense transit.

Rahu can bring fortunate opportunities to the partner but the over blown ego can cause distance and separation. The partner is away on travel or disconnected emotionally giving a sense of separation and isolation in a marriage or relationship.

There may be the need to escape the trials and tribulations that plague the life. There is a definite sense of feeling disconnected to the world or life's experiences. It may be time for a spiritual quest to understand new feelings of otherworldliness. Isolation and confusion give a sense of detachment. Giving off the feeling of a loner others sense the subtle energy and cannot find a connection.

Rahu transits the 8th; Ketu transits the 2nd

Rahu transiting the 8th house will cause highs and lows in financial matters, depending on planets and the sign in this house. Benefic planets in own signs or exalted in the 8th house will give financial gains. Family life may change with loss of family members, or divorce creates sorrow.

Gains in money may come from an unexpected inheritance or financial settlement. This pattern can also produce money from unearned sources such as divorce, taxes, or insurance policies.

Addictions or mental imbalances may cause emotional upsets and major problems if left unchecked. Feelings of suicide or depression must be addressed. Psychological analysis and treatment is a part of transformation and healing.

Loss of appetite will cause weight loss. The teeth may become loose and require dental work. There is a decline in eyesight; it may be time for glasses.

Rahu transits the 9th; Ketu transits the 3rd

A quest for higher knowledge inspires new studies in philosophy and spirituality. Your studies, plus the influence of good teachers, have the capacity to change the direction of your life. But don't place your entire trust in the hands of a guru-type figure because their intentions may not be entirely pure.

Education will be a passion, with a desire to obtain degrees. Unusual subjects inspire and open your mind. Thoughts along spiritual lines can give life a sense of meaning. There may be an interest in different cultures, and opportunities for travel to foreign places, perhaps as part of a spiritual pilgrimage.

Legal problems involving immigration or naturalization issues may need to be addressed.

Circumstances surrounding the father may be nagging at you, posing problems. At the very least, a health checkup for him is recommended. There may also be losses or separations involving a sibling.

Your willpower and drive are low, discouraging you from participating in physical activities. Depression can take a toll on the mind, resulting in a lackluster interest in life. Lack of mental focus may disrupt educational efforts.

Rahu transits the 10th; Ketu transits the 4th

Expect major changes in the career. There will be an overhaul at your place of work. It is transition time for your career, so a new type of work may be necessary.

A job loss or major career change can move life in a different direction, possibly entailing change of home or residence. You may find yourself spending more time away from home than you'd like to.

There are likely expenditures on the home or car. It's best not to purchase a home or car at this time. Even so, cars may cause major problems, breaking down or requiring significant repair.

There are security issues concerning home and family. Financial matters can also cause problems with self-esteem.

An emptiness in the heart may remind you that you need to feel a connection with home and family. Loss of, or problems with, the mother can bring family closer. Family reunions bring back memories and long-forgotten feelings. Although there's a wandering unsettled feeling in your soul, changes in residence are not permanent.

Rahu transits the 11th; Ketu transits the 5th

New influential acquaintances may encourage you to take a different direction. Powerful friends can give you opportunities. Social connections are the source of your new-found success.

This is a time of productivity gains and advancement in your career. Money in the form of bonuses or promotions may come in large payments.

Children are a source of trouble or concern. Be aware of their whereabouts and associations. There could be a separation from children, due to breakups in your marital status or their going away to college. Consequently, this could demand major expenses, eg, from divorce settlements or education costs.

You may experience amazing insights, with visions of future trends that could become lucrative. Be careful investing, however, because you may be overly zealous and optimistic. Obsessions from the past can take control of the mind in a negative way. Nevertheless, once the creative mind is awakened, it's time to explore new interests in the arts and creativity. It's time to write that book.

Rahu transits the 12th; Ketu transits the 6th

Unknown to you, there may be secret enemies, eg, hackers, scam artists, waiting to steal private information, so take the necessary precautions for your self-protection. Thieves may also be a cause of material losses. Avoid disreputable neighborhoods or places frequented by unsavory characters.

Rahu in the 12th can provoke loss of stamina or physical endurance. Mental or emotional stress can also deplete the immune system. Worrying may cause you to lose sleep, which creates a vicious cycle of low resistance and ongoing fatigue. You need to monitor your health through regular physical checkups.

The conditions around your workplace may be depressing, and you often need help but lack the necessary support. Lies may be spread about your character. Legal problems may appear, or you're taken surprise by someone's unethical behavior.

The loss of a special aunt or uncle may disrupt the family. There's a lackluster interest in life.

CHAPTER 10

Kala Sarpa Yoga

The Kala Sarpa yoga is a pattern involving Rahu and Ketu. This is an extremely powerful yoga that can't be ignored, and suggests a life of fate and destiny. It occurs when all the planets are on one side of the Rahu–Ketu axis. Even if a planet is in the same sign as Rahu and Ketu it still constitutes a Kala Sarpa yoga.

Note, however, that this only pertains to the planets visible to the naked eye, so Uranus, Neptune and Pluto aren't included. The outer planets are not personal planets, but represent the collective consciousness of the world.

Those with a Kala Sarpa yoga experience extreme highs and lows. Furthermore, any indications in the chart become even more potent. Once an individual goes through a difficult period, perhaps involving significant loss, they can rest assured they'll typically rebound with opportunities and improvements soon after. Life is a mystery that seems to be guided by a Divine force.

When any planet is conjunct Rahu or Ketu, with or without Kala Sarpa yoga, the effect of this planet becomes magnified. Planets conjunct Rahu are magnified in outwardly, manifesting in the physical world. Planets conjunct Ketu are magnified on the interior, giving deep perception and awareness.

If a planet is conjunct Rahu within a Kala Sarpa yoga, it's important to note whether Rahu is before or after that planet with respect to the direction Rahu is moving. Rahu and Ketu travel backwards in the zodiac. If the planet is in a lower zodiacal degree of the sign with Rahu, then the two are coming closer, so the planet is considered to be entering the mouth of Rahu. If the planet is in a higher zodiacal degree than Rahu, the two are separating, and the planet is considered to be in the tail or back of Rahu. If the latter, it means the planet has already been burned and destroyed. To be in the mouth of Rahu is not as destructive for a planet.

For a planet that has been burned, major problems throughout life are attributed to it. It is the focus of pain and suffering within a lifetime, involving some karmic issue from a previous life to be worked out. This issue can be discerned through the position of Ketu, suggesting where the karma originated in a previous life.

Wherever Ketu is by sign and house always indicates some desire to complete or finish something. But ironically, nothing ever feels complete because there's an overwhelming sense of emptiness that must be filled. This is because it was left incomplete in a previous lifetime.

The chart of Joseph Kennedy Senior is a prime example of the perils due to the Kala Sarpa yoga, since the planet that represented his children was in the tail or back of Rahu.

7th h.		8th h.		9th h.		10th h.	
				♅℞ 10:01 Roh			
				♀℞ 13:40 Roh			
6th h.		Joseph P. Kennedy Sr.				☊ 07:25 Pus	11th h.
		Thu 09-06-1888				♄ 22:13 Asl	
		07:06:00					
		Boston, Massachusetts					
5th h.	☋ 07:25 USh	USA				☉ 21:58 PPh	12th h.
		Timezone: 5 DST: 0				☽ 25:54 PPh	
		Latitude: 42N21'30					
		Longitude: 71W03'35					
		Ayanamsha : -22:17:54 Lahiri					
		♂ 04:51 Anu				☿ 03:41 UPh	
		♃ 07:06 Anu				♀ 07:30 UPh	
						ASC 12:44 Has	
						♆ 23:16 Has	
4th h.		3rd h.		2nd h.		1st h.	

145

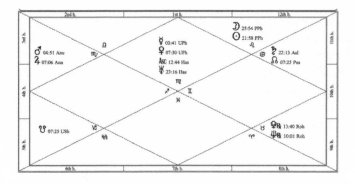

Saturn in his chart rules the 5th house of children. Because it's in a higher degree than Rahu, the two are separating, so it's considered to be in the tail of Rahu. Saturn also aspects the 5th house of children by opposition. Saturn and Rahu are in Cancer whose lord the Moon is in the 12th house of loss. Additionally, the Moon is conjunct the Sun which both occupies and rules the 12th house.

Ketu as the generic indicator for loss is in the 5th house of children. This all explains the extreme rise and fall of his famous children. His oldest son Joseph died in a plane crash during WW2. His oldest daughter Kathleen also died in a plane crash. His sons, President John F. Kennedy and Robert Kennedy, were both assassinated. So he witnessed the death of four of his children. He also had a retarded daughter, and his youngest son, Ted Kennedy, was disgraced in the Chappaquiddick scandal.

This is all just part of the extremes imposed upon him by the Kala Sarpa yoga. The most treacherous part, however, is that Saturn the lord of his 5th house was in the tail of Rahu. This means Saturn and its indications, eg, for children, are burned.

Sometimes, when Rahu is aspecting Jupiter (conjunct, opposed or trine) there can be issues or problems with children. This is due to Jupiter being the *karaka*, or significator for children in a chart. This is also a consideration in Joseph Kennedy's chart, since Rahu trines Jupiter. Other famous individuals who have Kala Sarpa yoga and Jupiter aspecting Rahu are Michael Milken who had two epileptic children, and Sylvester Stallone whose child died.

Michael Milken is an American stockbroker who amassed a fortune of $550 million in the 1980s through insider trading of junk bonds. His financial losses totaled $1.1 billion in fines and restitutions. While in prison he created a business for adult and children's education called *Knowledge Universe* which had sales of more than a $1 billion in 1997. This was definitely a major comeback after great destruction.

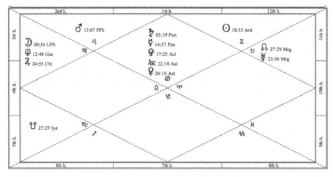

Sylvester Stallone is a famous movie star who became an overnight sensation with his hit movie *Rocky* about a struggling prizefighter. Stallone was a struggling actor who went on to great fame with many hit movies in Hollywood. His life has seen many highs and lows that can be attributed to this Kala Sarpa yoga.

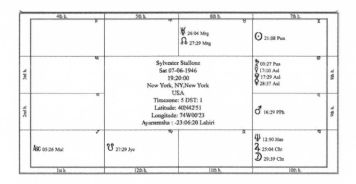

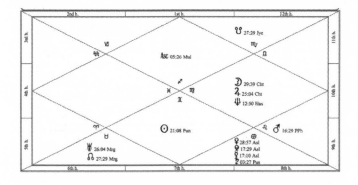

Another life full of extremes from the fated Kala Sarpa yoga is that of Christina Onassis, daughter of Aristotle Onassis, the Greek shipping tycoon and one of the richest men in the world. He married Jacqueline Kennedy, former wife of President John F. Kennedy. Christina lost her only brother to a plane crash but after her parents' deaths she inherited one of the world's largest fortunes. She had great difficulty with relationships, and by age 28 was married three times.

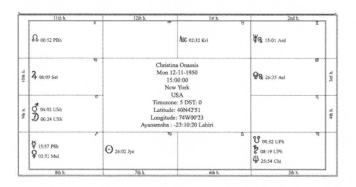

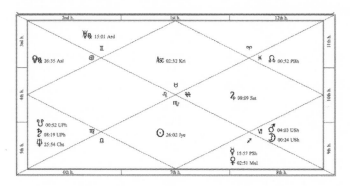

Christina's daughter Athina also has Kala Sarpa yoga and had great difficulties through rises and falls in her life. Her mother Christina died when she was only three years old. Although she became heir to the Onassis fortune, this massive wealth also brought her a multitude of troubles.

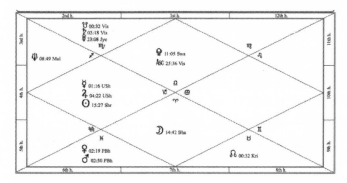

Famous people with Kala Sarpa yoga include: Donald Trump, George Bush Jr, Sylvester Stallone, Paul McCartney, Ringo Starr, Michael Milken, Joseph Kennedy Sr, Robert Kennedy, Christina Onassis and daughter Athina.

CHAPTER 11

Personal Planets conjunct Rahu and Ketu

In Vedic astrology the lunar nodes known as Rahu and Ketu have special powers in a chart. They influence our karmic destiny, indicating our greatest gifts and our darkest issues. In predictive work, the places where eclipses fall will indicate areas of our life that involve the most transformation that year.

When the lunar nodes are combined with another planet, they take on the quality of that planet, and magnify its energy. Each combination will produce amazing but very different results.

Rahu and Ketu are described as shadowy planets since they cause eclipses of the Sun and Moon. Out of their shadows came the powerful myths associated with the nodes, myths of struggles with demons, serpents and forces of darkness and light. Symbolically, they can also be seen as our own shadows.

In a birth chart, the extremes caused by Rahu and Ketu will influence:

1) The houses that Rahu and Ketu occupy.

2) The houses of their dispositors.

3) The houses ruled by the planet that conjoins Rahu or Ketu.

4) The nakshatra dispositors of Rahu and Ketu, and any planets in conjunction with them.

To get a deeper look at the results a planet will produce, you must look to the nakshatra dispositor of the planet. This is important, since the nakshatras are an integral element of Vedic astrology, and to ignore them would be to deny one of the key principles of Vedic astrology. The nakshatras govern the entire predictive system used in Vedic astrology, the Vimshottari dasha system. This system is based on the nakshatra your natal Moon occupies at birth. The nakshatra that rules the natal Moon launches the dasha cycle that determines the entire sequence of events in a lifetime.

Rahu and Ketu form Raja Yoga

Rahu and Ketu create a Raja Yoga (powerful positive combination) in either of two instances:

- Rahu or Ketu occupies a kendra (angular house: 1, 4, 7, or 10) while associated with a trikona lord, or

- Rahu or Ketu occupies a trikona (trinal house: 1, 5, or 9) while associated with a kendra lord.

Essentially this brings together the rulers, by location and house lordship, of kendra and trikona houses, just as in other Raja Yoga combinations.

For example, Donald Trump's Sun and Rahu conjunction create Raja Yoga since the Sun and Rahu are in an angular house (10th house) and the Sun rules the 1st house (Leo) which is also counted as a trinal house. Note, the 1st house functions as both a trikona and kendra. This empowers the Sun and Rahu in an even more substantive way, producing great results in his career, as President of the United States.

Effects of Rahu

Rahu (the Moon's north node) has the nature of a serpent. It poisons you with the illusions of this world. Our desires keep us reincarnating here. Rahu gives, but with a price. When our most intense desires are granted under Rahu, we discover that too much of a good thing can end up causing us suffering. For example, we may gain fame and fortune, only to realize we have no freedom, nowhere to go without being mauled by fans. Family and friends disown us out of jealousy. The fame and fortune we desired brings us separation and sorrow. Ultimately, disillusionment leads to enlightenment. But Ketu's influence detaches us, facilitates renunciation, and clears the way for spiritual enlightenment.

The nodes are the most powerful of all the planets because they cause the eclipses of the Sun and Moon. The nodes block out the light of consciousness. Rahu is the material world and the desires it creates. It gives material things which never bring lasting happiness. This is the illusion of Rahu. When these things start to fall away we become obsessed with trying to hold on to them. Rahu deals with fear, and obsessive or compulsive behavior. It's about addictions, poisons, alcohol, and drugs. Any planet with Rahu in the chart will become magnified since Rahu will take on the quality of the planet it is next to (in the same sign). This can be good or bad depending on the planet. Rahu with Venus or Jupiter can bring wealth, but Rahu with Saturn can cause suffering to the house they're in.

Keywords: Fame, status, prestige, power, worldly success, fulfillment of worldly desires, outer success with inner turmoil, extremes, obsessive behavior, addictions, psychic disturbances, collective trends, foreigners and foreign lands, epidemics, disease, poisons that destroy and heal, medicine, drugs and alcohol.

Rahu and Ketu take on the quality of the planets that are associated with them (especially conjunct) or aspect them. If they aren't associated with or aspected by other planets they'll give the results of the planet that rules the sign they're in (dispositor).

The sign and nakshatra dispositors are considered the karmic control planets.

Rahu and Ketu cast the trine aspect five and nine signs away from their position.

Rahu acts like Saturn, and Ketu acts like Mars. In my opinion, they can also be characterized as similar to the outer planets. Rahu is like Pluto or a mixture of Uranus/Saturn/Pluto, while Ketu is like Neptune or a mixture of Neptune/Mars/Uranus.

Rahu and Ketu will give raja yoga in either of these two situations: when they occupy a kendra and are conjunct a trinal ruler, or they occupy a trikona and are conjunct a kendra ruler.

Frequency of Rahu/Ketu conjunctions with planets

Conjunctions of the nodes and planets will always occur in the sign Rahu and Ketu transit during the 18-month period Rahu and Ketu are in a sign, once with Rahu and then with Ketu.

The Sun conjoins Rahu once a year (during an eclipse), six months apart.

The Moon conjoins Rahu once a month.

Mercury and Venus, once a year.

Mars, once every two years.

Jupiter, once every seven years, the conjunction typically occurring eight signs away from the previous conjunction.

Saturn, once every 11 years, the conjunction occurring six signs from the previous conjunction.

As we go through all the planets in conjunction with Rahu the qualities of each planet will be magnified.

The Sun conjunct Rahu

Sun (Surya): The Sun is the life force of our planet. It is the soul and spirit of a chart. However, it can be an overpowering influence. If it is too close to other planets it can burn up their capability to function properly. This condition is called combustion. The Sun works best in the tenth house where it gives a sense of power and career opportunity. In other houses its forceful presence can be excessive and cause problems.

Key Words: Atma (Self), masculine, day, future, soul, physical body and health, heart, life force, courage, pride, ego, vitality, willpower, stamina, sense of self, power, fame, glory, inspiration, creativity, leadership, father, teachers, authority, law and order, bosses, political leaders, kings or presidents.

The Sun is the karaka for the father and leaders or presidents.

Famous people with Sun conjunct Rahu:

- Hank Aaron: Sun conjunct Rahu, Saturn, and Venus in Capricorn in the 5th house

- Cheyenne Brando: Sun conjunct Rahu with Venus in Aquarius in the 10th house

- Elizabeth Kubler-Ross: Sun conjunct Rahu, Pluto and Moon in Gemini in the 5th house

- Timothy Leary: Sun conjunct Rahu and Mercury in Libra in the 12th house

- David Cassidy: Sun conjunct Rahu in Pisces in the 10th house

- Donald Trump: Sun conjunct Rahu in Taurus in the 10th house

Donald Trump's chart:

The Sun is the atma or the self. It is the ego and rules our motivations and drive in life. The Sun rules leaders, teachers and is the karaka of the father. With the Sun conjunct Rahu, his ego and sense of self-worth is expanded and exaggerated. In the 10th house this expands his career. He was arguably the most powerful man in New York City before venturing on to the most powerful position in the world as President of the United States. Because Rahu indicates expansion in the materialistic world, Trump's desire is for power, since the Sun in his chart rules the 1st house giving personal power. According to Parashara, Rahu is exalted in the sign of Taurus, thus giving it great power to fulfill the indications of the 10th house, ie, career and status. An exalted planet is in high form, giving it more power to produce the indications of the house occupied.

Rahu and the Sun are in the nakshatra Mrigashira ruled by Mars. Mars is in the 1st house of personal power. The nakshatra the planet and Rahu are in are equally as important as the sign. His ascendant and Mars are conjunct the fixed star Regulus, the star of kings and leaders.

He was born on a lunar eclipse, complicating his life with women and creating emotional issues due to relationships and marriage. This is because on a lunar eclipse the Sun and Moon are in opposition and conjunct the lunar nodes. The oppositions activate relationship issues, since they are 7th from one another.

When Trump entered into Rahu's cycle in 1999, his father died. The Sun is the karaka of the father, and Sun with Rahu signifies power and leadership. Rahu represents extremes and power. It will work as a malefic giving what is desired but with a price to be paid. When the nodes (either Rahu or Ketu) are conjunct a planet, and the person enters the dasha/bhukti of the planet and the node, such as when Trump entered into dasha/bhukti of Rahu/Sun, then an extreme result will manifest. It can be problematic for the person the planet is karaka for, as the Sun is the karaka for the father.

In 2016 he was elected President of the United States as transiting Jupiter was in trine to his Sun and Rahu in the 10th house.

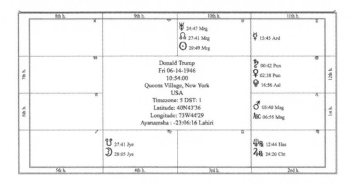

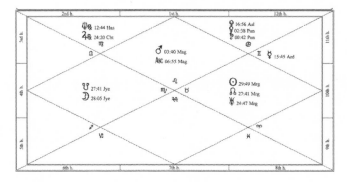

The Moon conjunct Rahu

Moon (Chandra): The Moon is the reflective influence. The Sun sends out its radiance and the Moon reflects it back. It is receptive, and therefore represents the reflective mind giving consciousness. The Moon is the nurturing, protecting influence that a mother provides. It is the Yin or female influence while the Sun is Yang or male.

Keywords: The mind, reflection, feminine, night, emotions, sensitivity, nurturing, security, past, past lives, patterns of behavior, receptivity, caring for others, heredity, mother, the public or masses, popularity, inner contentment, home, water, habits, subconscious mind.

The Moon is the karaka for the mother and the mind.

Famous people with Moon conjunct Rahu:

- Pamela Anderson: Moon and Rahu in Aries in the 12th house
- Tony Blair: Moon conjunct Rahu in Capricorn in the 10th house
- Gloria Vanderbilt: Moon conjunct Rahu in Leo in the 5th house
- Sharon Tate: Moon conjunct Rahu in Leo in the 3rd house
- Jacqueline Kennedy Onassis: Moon conjunct Rahu in Aries in the 7th house.

Jacqueline Kennedy Onassis' chart:

The Moon is the emotions and the mind. With Rahu it indicates an obsessive and compulsive mind. It will indicate a life with extremes interfering with peace of mind. The Moon and Rahu in the 7th house indicates the area of life this extreme tension will occur. The 7th house indicates the partner as in marriage or business. I see the 7th house as relationships that are contractual. The Moon rules the 10th house, indicating a relationship with the partner that is connected to her career or social standing. She was a very public figure who boosted her husband's career as the First Lady. When the 7th and 10th houses are connected the person will work in some capacity with the spouse.

Taking a deeper look, Rahu is in the nakshatra Bharani and it is ruled by Venus. Venus is in Taurus in the 8th house. The ruler of the 8th in the 8th house of death, ultimately predicts the death of the husband. The Moon is in Ashwini ruled by Ketu, and Ketu is in the 1st house, meaning the results of this planet will affect her personally.

At the time of the assassination of President Kennedy she was in the dasha of Moon-Rahu. They are both in the 7th house and the nakshatra dispositor of Rahu (Bharani) is Venus in the 8th house of death.

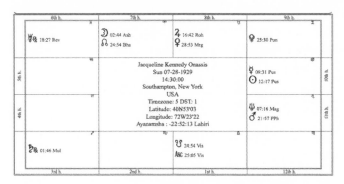

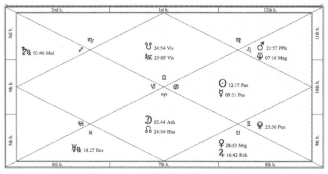

Mercury conjunct Rahu

Mercury (Budha): Generally, Mercury has to do with all forms of communication: speech, writing, and publications. Mercury also rules the intellect, learning, education, wit and a sense of humor. Mercury was the messenger of the gods and could travel to the underworld, the symbolic realm of hidden secrets where ordinary mortals couldn't enter. In Greek mythology, Hermes (Mercury) was also a trickster and a thief. Mercury's attributes include dexterity and creative ability with the hands. Mercury is fast and relates to short quick travels. He rules youthfulness and agelessness and is the perpetual Peter Pan, androgynous like a child before puberty.

Key Words: Communications, speech, writing, commerce, sales, education, ideas, thoughts, school, analytical mind, rational mind, cognitive intelligence, sense of humor, youth, trickster, truth, telephones, television, computers, short distance travel, adaptability, childhood, aunts and uncles, neighbors, twins.

Mercury is the karaka for aunts and uncles, communications and intellect.

Famous people with Mercury conjunct Rahu:

- Errol Flynn: Mercury conjunct Rahu in Taurus in the 2nd house
- Jacques Cousteau: Mercury Conjunct Rahu and Sun in Taurus in the 9th house
- Yoko Ono: Mercury conjunct Rahu and Sun in Aquarius in the 6th house
- Al Capone: Mercury conjunct Rahu in Sagittarius in the 11th house
- Jackie Gleason: Mercury conjunct Rahu in Capricorn in the 2nd house

- Edgar Cayce: Mercury conjunct Rahu, Saturn and Venus in Aquarius in the 8th house

Edgar Cayce's chart:

Edgar Cayce was the most prolific psychic of the 20th century. He would give information in trance medium sessions. His Mercury/Rahu conjunction in the 8th house gives him his psychic abilities. Mercury rules the 3rd and the 12th house. The 12th house relates to spirituality and the 3rd house is communications. With Mercury in the 8th house his spirituality and communication skills come from his psychic ability. Both Mercury and Rahu are in the nakshatra Shatabhishak, which is ruled by Rahu. This makes Rahu even more powerful in its own nakshatra. It is like a planet in its own sign of rulership.

On March 16th, 1886, Cayce had his first vision. Two years later he was pronounced dead from drowning, but recovered. He was in Venus-Mercury when he had his first vision. Both planets are in the 8th house in Aquarius ruled by Saturn. All these planets, Venus, Saturn, Mercury and Rahu are in the 8th house. Rahu actually intensifies all these planets, giving him his amazing psychic abilities.

But the 8th house is also the house of difficulty and death. He was in Venus-Ketu during the time of his near-death experience with drowning. Venus is in the 8th house and Ketu is in the 2nd house, a maraka house, indicating possible death. But most importantly, Ketu is in Purva Phalguni ruled by Venus, and Venus is again in the 8th house, and it is in Aquarius ruled by Saturn. Venus' nakshatra is ruled by Saturn, ruler of the 8th house in the 8th house. All these planets in the 8th house are intensified in the 8th house of death and psychic ability. When he died January 3rd, 1945, he'd just entered into Saturn's mahadasha.

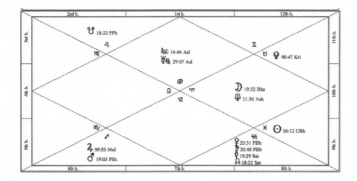

Venus conjunct Rahu

Venus (Shukra): Venus is the principle of attraction and therefore rules relationships. Relationships result in procreation and Venus is creative energy and passion. This not only relates to children but to all forms of the creative arts. It rules the senses and the pleasures of the physical body, which also include taste, music, touch, luxuries and aesthetic beauty. Venus refers to a person's wealth and to their comforts in life.

Keywords: The feminine spirit, beauty, grace, charm, refinement, luxuries, wealth, sensuality, vanity, charisma, glamour, good taste, sexual attraction, elegance, comforts, conveyances, arts, music, theater, love, affections, pleasure of the senses, sugar, flowers, the wife in a male's chart.

Venus is the karaka of relationships, luxuries, and the wife in a man's chart.

Famous people with Venus conjunct Rahu:

- Burt Reynolds: Venus conjunct Rahu in Sagittarius in the 8th house
- Sigmund Freud: Venus conjunct Rahu in Aries in the 7th house
- Merv Griffin: Venus conjunct Rahu and Mercury and Mars in Cancer in the 2nd house
- Catherine Oxenberg: Venus conjunct Rahu in Leo in the 3rd house
- Ted Kennedy: Venus Conjunct Rahu in Pisces in the 4th house
- Elvis Presley: Venus conjunct Rahu in Capricorn in the 3rd house

Elvis Presley's chart:

Rahu and Venus together represent extremes in the area of beauty, wealth and luxuries. Venus and Rahu in the sign of Capricorn represent leadership and business affairs. Venus and Rahu are in the 3rd house indicating extreme talent in communication skills. It is the house of siblings. Elvis had a twin brother who died at birth. Venus rules the 7th and 12th houses indicating extreme losses in the area of the 3rd house. The 7th house is a difficult house being a maraka house. The 12th house indicates loss. The sign dispositor of Venus and Rahu is Saturn placed in the 4th house. He was a very private person. The fame and notoriety forced him further inward. He spent a lot of time alone at home. He was very close to his mother, but in a very obsessive way since Saturn is the dispositor of Venus and Rahu.

Venus and Rahu in Uttara Ashadha, because Saturn is in Dhanishta in the 4th house, which is ruled by the Sun. The Sun is in the 2nd house representing his powerful voice that made him a legend and gave him the title "the King." The 2nd house is the voice and wealth, in which the Venus/Rahu would predict the extremes produced from these houses.

On the day of his death, 08/16/1977 he was in Saturn-Moon, both in the 4th house which is considered the house of the end of life. Saturn is the sign dispositor of Rahu/Venus and the Moon is in Shatabhishak ruled by Rahu. This connects the Venus/Rahu in the 3rd house, which the 3rd house is also a house of death, being the 8th from the 8th house using *bhavat bhavam*.

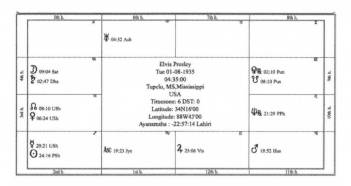

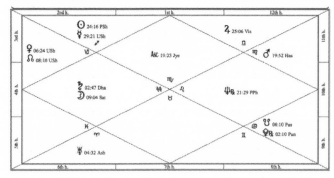

Mars conjunct Rahu

Mars (Mangala): Mars is the commander in chief. He is the planet of war. Mars rules the blood and the circulation of life force in the body. Mars' nature is fiery and if provoked, he will fight. Mars deals with issues of anger but is also the planet of ambition and zest for life. It brings out suppressed energies or inner turmoil. Mars is very impulsive, aggressive and impatient; it represents accidents, surgery, wars, and volcanic eruptions, with courage and fearlessness as its positive side.

Keywords: Energy, action, passions, fire, blood, sexual vitality, male influence, muscles, athletics, courage, strength, determination, motivation, self-righteousness, selfishness, anger, violence, aggression, injury, accidents, enemies, war, can inflict death, conflict, military, police, criminals, science, machines, weapons, guns, knives, property and real estate, brothers.

Mars is the karaka, for brothers (siblings), intelligence and real estate.

Famous people with Mars conjunct Rahu:

- John Adams: Mars conjunct Rahu in Virgo in the 1st house
- Clint Eastwood: Mars conjunct Rahu in Aries in the 7th house
- Harry Houdini: Mars conjunct Rahu in Aries in the 3rd house
- Joan Crawford: Mars conjunct Rahu in Virgo in the 12th house
- Carolyn Myss: Mars conjunct Rahu in Capricorn in the 3rd house
- Jerry Seinfeld: Mars conjunct Rahu in Sagittarius in the 9th house

- Albert Einstein: Mars conjunct Rahu in Capricorn in the 8th house

Albert Einstein's chart:

Mars and Rahu occupy the 8th house, intensifying the qualities of the 8th house. Mars is exalted in Capricorn, giving it even more intensity. The 8th house indicates deep profound thoughts and research. Mars is the planet of intelligence, so together with Rahu in the thought-provoking 8th house we have a brilliant mind who uncovers answers to the Universe.

Rahu is in Shravana which is ruled by the Moon, and the Moon is in the 6th house. This indicates his prodding scientific mind, searching for answers. His Mars is in Uttara Ashadha which is ruled by the Sun. The Sun in the 10th house gave him fame and recognition, particularly due to his scientific discoveries.

Saturn is the sign dispositor of Rahu and Mars. It is in the 10th house of career and social recognition which did come about later in his life. In 1922 he won the Nobel Prize, he was in Moon-Mars. The Moon is in Scorpio ruled by Mars, and Mars is with Rahu in the 8th house.

Mars, the planet conjunct Rahu, takes on this magnification and activates the houses it rules. Mars rules the 11th and the 6th houses. These are the houses of healing. But since Mars is in the 8th house he felt he had a lot to do with the destruction of many lives. He had enormous guilt dealing with the outcome of his discovery and development of nuclear energy. He didn't create it for destruction, but this was exactly how it was used.

He died of an aortic aneurism in 1955 when he was in Rahu-Mars dasha. Both these intensified planets are in the 8th house of death. There is no surprise this is the dasha that took his life.

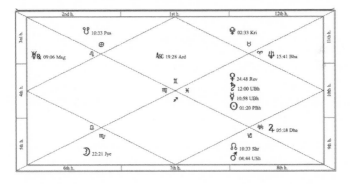

Jupiter conjunct Rahu

Jupiter (Guru): Jupiter is the preceptor and teacher of the gods. He was to teach the path of righteousness and spiritual wisdom and represents God's grace. Jupiter is expansion and growth. Whatever Jupiter aspects will grow large. This can indicate overweight conditions or a tall stature. Even an expanded organ such as the liver can cause health difficulties. Jupiter deals with the external rituals associated with religion. It is also about judgment and laws pertaining to legal advice and it rules lawyers.

Keywords: Spiritual teacher, guide, truth, faith, religion, philosophy, spirituality, grace, law, the great benefic, fortune, wealth, expansion, higher education like colleges, optimism, generosity, joy, luck, self-indulgence, excess, money, long distance travel, children, the husband in a female's chart.

The karakas for Jupiter are children, the spouse in a woman's chart and wealth.

Famous people with Jupiter conjunct Rahu:

- Roger Daltrey: Jupiter conjunct Rahu in Cancer in the 9th house
- Ursula Andress: Jupiter conjunct Rahu in Sagittarius in the 6th house
- Jill Ireland: Jupiter conjunct Rahu in Sagittarius in the 4th house
- Michael Landon: Jupiter conjunct Rahu in Sagittarius in the 1st house
- Scott Peterson: Jupiter conjunct Rahu in Sagittarius in the 2nd house
- Ellen Degeneres: Jupiter conjunct Rahu in Libra in the 12th house
- Madonna: Jupiter conjunct Rahu in Libra in the 3rd house

Madonna's chart:

Rahu and Jupiter are in the 3rd house which denotes great creative abilities. The sign Libra can indicate creativity, particularly with music, because Venus as ruler of Libra rules the arts, and air signs can indicate music. Venus as the sign dispositor of both Jupiter and Rahu is in the 12th house. The 12th house has connections to film and dancing. The 12th house is connected to film for the association to Neptune and Pisces, and the 12 house rules the feet, indicating dancing abilities.

Jupiter rules the 8th and the 5th houses. The 5th is another house of creativity and the 8th house indicates sex and magnetism. The ruler of the 8th house is magnified with Rahu producing a very charismatic individual.

The nakshatra dispositor of Chitra is Mars. Mars is in the 9th house in Aries. This gives her a lucky rise and her passion towards her religious beliefs. She was born in an Italian Catholic family and is now studying the Kabbalah. The nakshatra Chitra denotes someone who shines and stands out in a crowd.

Mars becomes a wild card being with Ketu. It is related to the Jupiter/Rahu because Mars/Ketu aspect Jupiter/Rahu, and Jupiter and Rahu's nakshatra dispositor is Mars. Jupiter and Rahu indicate expansion and huge extremes. Jupiter and Rahu magnetize the Mars/Ketu.

From 1987-1994 she was in Mars dasha. This was the time she rose to the top as one of the most popular performers, taking the world by a storm. She became an icon at this time. During her Mars-Ketu in 1991-1992 she produced the provocative taboo work "Truth or Dare", a video, and published the book "Sex". Madonna capitalized on her shock value, knowing the more shocking it was, the more she would be a public commodity. Someone with Mars and Ketu in the 9th house is not afraid to express their beliefs, no matter who it offends.

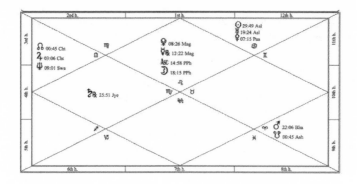

Saturn conjunct Rahu

Saturn (Shani): Saturn is the furthest planet visible to the naked eye. It is therefore the slowest and darkest from our perception (outer planets excluded here) and perceived as giving darkness, delaying or slowing things down. Saturn rules old age. It is the final boundary, suggesting death and doom. As one becomes disillusioned with life, there is misery and frustration. It is the function of Saturn to strip away everything of this existence to rid one of all desires and attachments. This eventually leads to higher consciousness and final liberation from the karmic chains of the world. Saturn's primary function is to lead the soul back to its source, to God. Characteristics of Saturn are delays, depression, restrictions, setbacks, destruction, disease and death. But Saturn also exhibits discipline, stability, and gives long lasting results.

Keywords: Discipline, order, structure, dependability, stability, concentration, endurance, longevity, separation, solitude, limitation, bondage, obstruction, delay, poverty, death, disease, oppression, pessimism, worry, doubt, fear, phobias, bad luck, old age, retardation, paralysis, depression, stunted development, deprivation, bones, skin, degenerative diseases, arthritis, fixed assets, land, property, darkness, sorrow, detachment, decay.

The karakas for Saturn are elderly people, death and wisdom.

Famous people with Saturn conjunct Rahu:

- Carnie Wilson: Saturn conjunct Rahu in Pisces in the 6th house
- Ashley Judd: Saturn conjunct Rahu and Venus in Pisces in the 8th house
- Judy Garland: Saturn conjunct Rahu and Jupiter in Virgo in the 4th house
- Timothy McVeigh: Saturn conjunct Rahu and Venus in Pisces in the 10th house
- David Copperfield: Saturn conjunct Rahu in Scorpio in the 3rd house
- Lisa Marie Presley: Saturn conjunct Rahu in Pisces in the 9th house
- Priscilla Presley: Saturn conjunct Rahu in Gemini in the 7th house

Priscilla Presley's chart:

She has Saturn/Rahu in the 7th house indicating the spouse. The relationship with Elvis no doubt changed her life in a huge way. It represents fame and destiny through the spouse. Interestingly in her daughter's chart, Lisa Marie has the same Saturn/Rahu conjunction in her 9th house of the father.

In Priscilla's chart Saturn rules the 2nd and 3rd houses. Saturn's magnification from Rahu brought the extremes of money from the 2nd house. The 3rd house indicates creative talents, and Priscilla came through with her acting abilities, but doors opened due to her famous marriage.

Mercury is the sign dispositor of Saturn and Rahu. In the 5th house it connects her to her children and represents fame still associated with her spouse.

The nakshatra of Saturn and Rahu is Ardra, which is ruled by Rahu. This intensifies Rahu even more, further intensifying the effect of her extreme blessing or curse she experienced through her marriage to one of the most famous people of our time. Ardra is a nakshatra associated with tragic events.

In 1977 when Priscilla was in the Saturn-Rahu period, Elvis Presley died. Once again the relevance and power of this combination predicted this unexpected shocking event.

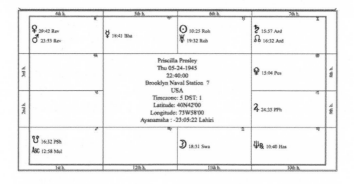

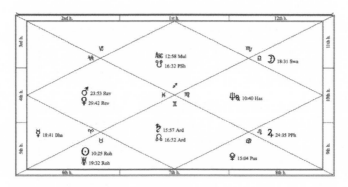

Lisa Marie Presley's chart:

She has Saturn and Rahu in Pisces in the 9th house indicating the extremes in life came from the father. Saturn rules the 8th and 7th houses. The 8th house has to do with inheritances, whereby she inherited most of her father's fortune. The sign dispositor of Rahu and Saturn is Jupiter in the 2nd house. This further indicates the wealth gained from the father.

Saturn is in Uttara Bhadrapada ruled by Saturn. This is like Saturn in its own sign, strengthening the power of Saturn. Rahu is in Revati which is ruled by Mercury. Mercury in the 8th house indicates the lack of the father in her life. He died before she really got to know him. He was not a part of her life.

At the time of her father's death, Lisa was in the Saturn-Ketu period. Natal Saturn is in the 9th house and the nakshatra dispositor is Saturn, and Saturn rules the 8th house of death. The nakshatra dispositor and sign dispositor of Ketu are both in the 8th house. Ketu is in Virgo, the sign dispositor is Mercury, and Ketu is in the nakshatra Chitra, which is ruled by Mars, so Mars is the nakshatra dispositor. Both Mercury and Mars are in the 8th house in Saturn's sign. A major focus of these two planets' conjoined periods (Saturn-Ketu) are 8th house matters dealing with 9th house matters, therefore death of the father.

173

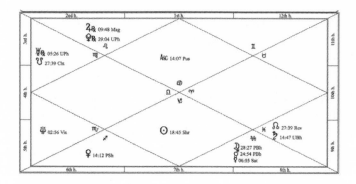

Effects of Ketu

Ketu (Moon's south node): Ketu's function is to cause inner turmoil so that the soul will seek the true essence of the individual. Whereas Rahu is the material world, Ketu is the spiritual world. It is the headless serpent, implying the perception and wisdom that is a gut-level knowing that can give psychic or clairvoyant abilities. But Ketu can give a feeling of helplessness, self-doubt and lack of confidence. Through humiliating experiences one becomes humble. Ketu is a wanderer without roots. It is a fiery force that can cause accident and injury. Above all, it is the karaka of loss that directs our attention back to the eternal reality, the self-realization of our essence with God. Rahu works on the outer material world and Ketu works on the inner spiritual world.

Ketu with a planet will have a spiritualizing effect on it, directing the planetary energy to look within its essence. If Ketu is with Mars, the nature will actively seek the spiritual side of life; Martian qualities will be withdrawn, anger suppressed and channeled inwardly. Ketu with the Moon can give psychic abilities. Like Rahu, Ketu can cause mental instabilities, mass hysteria, diseases and plagues, and represent poisons like drugs and alcohol. However, both Rahu and Ketu can also indicate drugs or poisons that heal.

174

Keywords: Loss, negation, lack of confidence, self-doubt, fantasies, confusion, indecision, illusions, drug addiction and alcoholism, psychic influences, fire, injury, death, spiritual insight, liberation, perception, wisdom.

There is an ambition for power wherever Ketu is positioned by house. The ambition for power comes from a strong empty feeling. The house it is in will feel like a void, creating an obsession to refill the emptiness. This is why there can be gains and abundance for the house that Ketu is in.

Ketu has been said to negate the planet it is conjunct or aspects. A planet conjunct Ketu becomes magnified in an unusual way, the outcome depending on the houses ruled by the planet with Ketu. Whether the planet with Ketu is a friend or enemy to the chart depends on the Ascendant.

Ketu is the suction point for all incoming karma from past incarnations. This karma is processed, then set forth through our life with experiences indicated by Rahu. Rahu is the future and new karmas developed during this lifetime. The controlling planets are the sign and nakshatra dispositors of Rahu and Ketu. Planets conjunct these nodes become the wild cards to express this experience even more. So Ketu is the past karmas of the soul which are put forth into action in this lifetime through Rahu. Ketu represents the talents and faculties developed through past lives. Ketu deals with the inheritance of these natural abilities but the real test is to balance these abilities and not let them control us. We must reach out and develop the Rahu qualities instead of letting the karma repeat itself from previous lifetimes. We must learn to use this power for the good of mankind instead of selfish self-grandeur. Ketu is our past while Rahu is our future and where we must develop our skills in this lifetime.

If Ketu is with a benefic planet the qualities of that house are empowered. If they are in the sign the planet rules, extremes of wealth are possible, especially in the mahadasha of Ketu.

For example, if Ketu is in the 2nd house with Jupiter it gives wealth. But if Ketu and Jupiter are in Sagittarius or Pisces, it gives extremes of wealth.

This becomes activated when Ketu's mahadasha begins. At the end of the seven-year Ketu cycle all the gains during this cycle can be lost.

Note: Planets conjunct Ketu will be exaggerated in an unusual way. The exaggeration is due to a sense of lack that is overcompensated.

Sun conjunct Ketu

Famous people with Sun conjunct Ketu:

- Nicolas Cage: Sun conjunct Ketu in Sagittarius in the 1st house
- Amelia Earhart: Sun conjunct Ketu in Cancer in the 4th house
- Chandra Levy: Sun conjunct Ketu in Aries in the 10th house
- Mike Love: Sun conjunct Ketu in Pisces in the 10th house
- Alice Bailey: Sun conjunct Ketu in Gemini in the 12th house
- Roman Polanski: Sun conjunct Ketu in Leo in the 12th house

Roman Polanski's chart:

He was an iconic movie producer. Twice in his life he was exiled from the countries he lived in. In 1939 his family had to flee Poland due to the German invasion of World War II. Then in 1977 he was exiled from the United States due to his indiscretion with minors in his love affairs.

An event that caused great loss and pain was in August 1969, when his wife Sharon Tate was brutally murdered in the Charles Manson murders. These are all effects of the karmas of the 12th house.

He has Sun conjunct Ketu in Leo in the 12th house. The intensity of this combination is stressed further by the sign and nakshatra rulers. Sun and Ketu are in Leo, where the Sun is the ruler of the 12th in the 12th house. Both Sun and Ketu are in Magha ruled by Ketu. This intensifies Ketu again, the ruler of the 12th in the 12th, where Ketu is the karaka of loss. The 12th house is the house of foreign lands, and Polanski was exiled twice in his life from the counties he lived in. This configuration brought about intense losses in his life.

The Sun indicates our ego and self-esteem, and with Ketu can mean the loss of these. The experiences in his life were humiliating and represent a deep sense of loss.

In 1977 when Polanski was exiled from the United States because of his scandalous affairs he was in Ketu-Rahu period. Ketu is powerfully connected to loss. Additionally, its placement in the 12th house indicates problems with foreign countries.

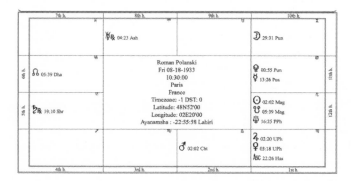

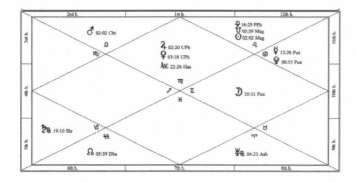

Moon conjunct Ketu

Famous people with Moon conjunct Ketu:

- Van Cliburn: Moon conjunct Ketu in Cancer in the 11th house
- Julia Child: Moon conjunct Ketu in Virgo in the 5th house
- Emeril Lagasse: Moon conjunct Ketu in Pisces in the 6th house
- John Paul Getty: Moon conjunct Ketu in Libra in the 11th house
- Barbra Mandrell: Moon conjunct Ketu in Libra in the 11th house
- Donald Trump: Moon conjunct Ketu in the 4th house
- Bobby Kennedy: Moon conjunct Ketu in Capricorn in the 10th house

Robert (Bobby) Kennedy's chart:

He has Moon/Ketu in the 10th house of career, fame and recognition. The Moon in the 10th house can represent fame, particularly with a node of the Moon. The Moon is the karaka of the masses, the public and the mother. Since the Moon rules the 4th house of the mother it indicates great loss for the mother. Rose Kennedy did lose almost all of her children tragically while she was still living. Moon and Ketu, which is located in the 7th house of marriage and partnerships. Saturn rules both the 10th and 11th houses, connecting Robert to his older brothers in business partnerships. The 11th house represents older siblings. The nakshatra of both Moon and Ketu is Uttara Ashadha which is ruled by the Sun. The Sun is powerfully placed in the 8th house. Therefore, his connections with his family, specifically his brothers, led him to great loss through Ketu, and eventually death through the nakshatra dispositor the Sun in the 8th house. He never got to fulfill his political desires for he had a greater destiny to fulfill for the world.

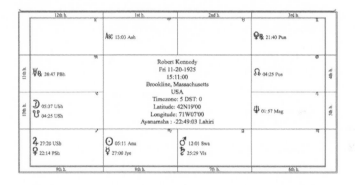

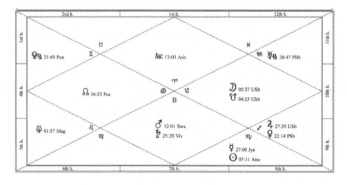

Mercury conjunct Ketu

Famous people with Mercury conjunct Ketu:

- Patrick Swayze: Mercury conjunct Ketu with Moon and Pluto in Cancer in the 11th house

- Alice Bailey: Mercury conjunct Ketu with Sun in Gemini in the 12th house

- Pope John Paul II: Mercury conjunct Ketu and Venus in Aries in the 9th house

- Phil Hartman: Mercury conjunct Ketu and Mars in Libra in the 10th house

- Cameron Diaz: Mercury conjunct Ketu in Cancer in the 2nd house

- Jon Bon Jovi: Mercury conjunct Ketu, Saturn, Mars, and Moon in Capricorn in the 5th house

- Howard Dean: Mercury conjunct Ketu in Libra in the 5th house

- Bobby Fischer: Mercury conjunct Ketu in Aquarius in the 8th house

Bobby Fischer's chart:

He became the world chess champion on 09/02/1972. He was exiled from the United States for his antagonistic behavior. After 20 years of exile he won $3.35 million in a rematch with Boris Spassky from Russia on 09/02/1992. He has the combination of Mercury with Ketu in the 8th house. The 8th house is the most profound house for thoughts and research. There are other aspects that denote his keen intelligence, but I believe it is the Mercury/Ketu in the 8th house that gave him his probing mind.

Mercury with Ketu indicates a deep mind, and in the 8th house gives the quality of concentration coupled with research, as Einstein had Mars/Rahu in the 8th house. Mercury in an air sign gives more of a mental quality. Mercury, the planet conjunct Ketu, rules the 12th and 3rd houses. The 3rd house indicates mental ability and communication skills, related to Mercury, which rules the 3rd sign, Gemini. The sign dispositor is Saturn. Saturn in the 11th house magnifies the results of Mercury/Ketu.

The 11th house magnifies and multiplies the results of planets. The nakshatra dispositor of Mercury is Mars (Dhanishta). Mars is exalted in the 7th house. Mars is the key planet for intelligence, as the dispositor exalted in an angle will give the extreme of Mars in all its glory. It is called Ruchaka Yoga. It probably had a lot to do with his antagonistic behavior.

In 1972 when he won the championship he was in the Moon-Mars period. Mars is his powerhouse and the Moon is in Mars' sign but the nakshatra that rules the Moon is Ketu (Ashwini), therefore the 8th house and Mercury are activated, giving depth to the thinking process.

9th h.	10th h.	11th h.	12th h.
♀ 22:07 Rev	☽ 09:01 Ash	♅ 07:54 Kri ♄ 13:26 Roh	♃℞ 22:07 Pun
☉ 25:18 PBh ☿ 04:47 Dha ☊ 01:43 Dha	**Bobby Fischer** Tue 03-09-1943 14:39:00 Chicago, Illinois USA Timezone: 6 DST: 1 Latitude: 41N51'00 Longitude: 87W39'00 Ayanamsha : -23:03:39 Lahiri		ASC 07:30 Pus ♀℞ 12:11 Pus
♂ 07:54 USh			☋ 01:43 Mag
			♆℞ 07:58 UPh
6th h.	5th h.	4th h.	3rd h.

181

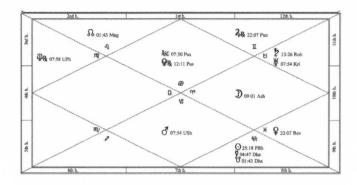

Venus conjunct Ketu

Famous people with Venus conjunct Ketu:

- Marcia Clark: Venus conjunct Ketu and Mars in Cancer in the 10th house
- William Randolph Price: Venus conjunct Ketu in Taurus in the 1st house
- Christian Dior: Venus conjunct Ketu in Aquarius in the 5th house
- Sammy Davis Jr. Venus conjunct Ketu with Jupiter in Capricorn in the 11th house
- Charles de Gaulle: Venus conjunct Ketu and Mercury/Sun in Scorpio in the 3rd house
- Conner Clapton: Venus conjunct Ketu in Virgo in the 2nd house
- Roger Daltrey: Venus conjunct Ketu in Capricorn in the 3rd house

Roger Daltrey's chart:

As the lead singer of the rock band "The Who", he has Venus conjunct Ketu in Capricorn in the 3rd house of creativity and communication skills. Roger's success is due to many aspects of this powerful chart, but

182

particularly his exalted Jupiter conjunct Rahu in the 9th house. The rise of "The Who" began in the 60s when he was in Rahu's cycle. In 1964 the group changed their name from "The Detours" to "The Who", and added Keith Moon as the drummer. He began his Rahu-Jupiter period. This catapulted them to fame and fortune.

His Venus and Ketu in the 3rd house is what gave him his creative exuberant style with entertaining on stage. In 1975 he began his acting career in the movie "Tommy". He was in Rahu-Venus. The 3rd house has indications of film and showmanship.

Venus rules the 7th and 12th houses. The sign dispositor Saturn is in the 7th house, also the nakshatra dispositor (Shravana) is the Moon. All these indications point to the 7th house. This confirms it was the group effort that made the "The Who" the success that it was. He has Saturn, Mars, and the Moon (with Uranus) in the 7th house.

One can see each of these planets as representing each of the other three members of the group. I see the Moon as Keith Moon, because he was the most fluctuating, and the Moon is close to planet Uranus, indicating emotional instability. He died at age 32 of a drug overdose in 1978. Besides, his last name is Moon! John Entwistle is represented by Mars, and Pete Townsend by Saturn.

Whenever I see three or more planets in the 7th house I know the individual is a success through the support of others, but also they are the ones who control and run the group. They get many people to help and do work for them. The combination of Saturn, Mars and Moon/Uranus describes the volatile relationships within the group.

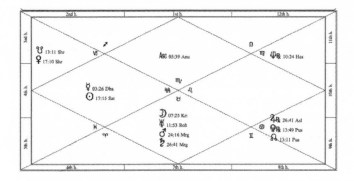

Mars conjunct Ketu

Famous people with Mars conjunct Ketu:

- David Cassidy: Mars conjunct Ketu in Virgo in the 4th house
- Karen Carpenter: Mars conjunct Ketu in Virgo in the 4th house
- Madonna: Mars conjunct Ketu in Aries in the 9th house
- Ted Bundy: Mars conjunct Ketu and the Moon, Sun and Mercury in Scorpio in the 4th house

- Kurt Cobain: Mars conjunct Ketu in Libra in the 3rd house
- George Gershwin: Mars conjunct Ketu in Gemini in the 8th house
- Brad Pitt: Mars conjunct Ketu and Mercury, Moon, and Sun in Sagittarius in the 2nd house
- Mark Spitz: Mars conjunct Ketu in Virgo in the 2nd house

Mark Spitz's Chart:

Mark won seven gold medals at the 1972 Olympics. He has Mars and Ketu in Virgo in the 2nd house. The sign Virgo denotes discipline and focus and in the 2nd house refers to his early childhood. His parents made Mark their focus, training him in swimming since a young age. He began breaking records as soon as he hit the water. His parents were so involved in his swimming career they moved three times to be close to better coaches. So close to Ketu, Mars becomes a driving force. Ketu can have the effects of Mars so together they become more intense.

The 2nd house indicates speech and eating which were extreme in both cases. He was noted for his particular eating habits, and disliked for his arrogant comments. His teammates made fun of him and called him a hypochondriac. Ultimately he made his fortune through endorsements arising from his success as an Olympic star. The 2nd house rules our ability to make our own money. Mars rules the 4th and 9th house indicating both the mother and father, and both parents made him their focus, sacrificing everything for his success.

The sign dispositor of Mars is Mercury which is placed in the 6th house of competition and improvement. This is a house involved with athletes. Also, whenever there's a connection between the 2nd and 6th house, one becomes vested in health matters, especially what they eat. The nakshatra dispositor of Hasta is the Moon. The Moon in the 4th house indicates the importance his mother had in his career.

He was in Mars-Ketu, April 1972-September 1972. So it was the Mars-Ketu period that prepared and brought him the triumph of one of the most successful Olympic wins in history, aside from the later record-breaker Michael Phelps of the 2008 Olympics.

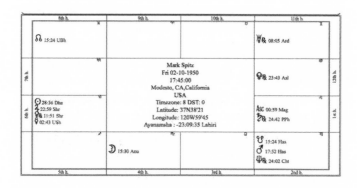

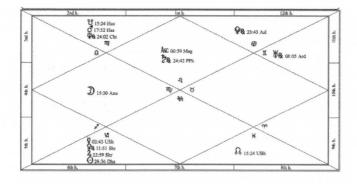

Jupiter conjunct Ketu

Famous people with Jupiter conjunct Ketu:

- Jennifer Aniston: Jupiter conjunct Ketu in Virgo in the 12th house

- Lucille Ball: Jupiter conjunct Ketu in Libra in the 11th house

- Hillary R. Clinton: Jupiter conjunct Ketu in Scorpio in the 6th house

- Steffi Graf: Jupiter conjunct Ketu in Virgo in the 4th house

- Henry David Thoreau: Jupiter conjunct Ketu in Scorpio in the 11th house

- Vincent Van Gogh: Jupiter conjunct Ketu in Sagittarius in the 7th house

- Jerry Seinfeld: Jupiter conjunct Ketu in Gemini in the 3rd house

Jerry Seinfeld's chart:

He is the highest paid TV comedian of our time. In terms of what constitutes being humorous in a chart I usually refer to the sign Gemini. To be funny you have to be smart and quick-witted, because your mind has to think quickly and be ahead of everyone in a conversation. Mercury is the trickster of Greek mythology and rules the mental disposition. In Gemini the mind is quick and adaptable. Virgo, also ruled by Mercury, produces a dry humor. Great comedians need a strong Mercury. Seinfeld has Jupiter in Gemini in the 3rd house. Jupiter is accentuated by Ketu in the 3rd house. The 3rd house is about communications and the arts, and Jerry has a talent to come across dramatically in his stage act.

Jupiter is magnified by Ketu and rules the 9th and the 12th houses. The 9th house gives him the popularity and blessings to be successful with his act. As Mars/Rahu aspect his Jupiter/Ketu configuration it becomes all the more magnified.

Mercury is the sign dispositor and resides in the 1st house of the self. This gives him a youthful appearance and flexible style. Mercury is in Aries with the exalted Sun, giving him drive, ambition and success. The Sun rules the 5th house of drama and creativity. Talented actors, artists, musicians and writers typically have accentuated 3rd and 5th houses.

The nakshatra dispositor of Jupiter is Mars, which rules Mrigashira. Mars is in the 9th house with Rahu aspecting his Jupiter/Ketu configuration, so it gives enormous power. The 3/9 house axis is great for communications on a public level. The 3rd house also rules media and television. Ketu is in Punarvasu ruled by Jupiter, so it accentuates his Jupiter even more. This is a magnificently magnified Jupiter. This is the powerhouse that gifted him with his humor, communication skills and drama.

He had his rise as a stand-up comedian during his Mercury dasha. The top-rated TV series "Seinfeld" ran from 1989 to 1998. As soon as he hit his Ketu dasha the show ended. He was ready to retire while at the top. He said he didn't need any more money, and wanted his freedom. I'm sure he traveled and had fun during this Ketu dasha.

Coincidentally, he has a Lakshmi yoga for wealth. Venus in its own sign (placed in the 2nd house), the ruler of the 9th house is aspected by the ruler of the 1st, and the ruler of the 1st is strong.

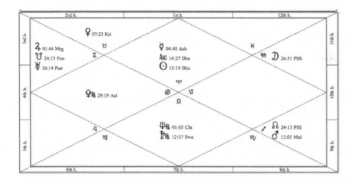

Saturn conjunct Ketu

Famous people with Saturn conjunct Ketu:

- Ralph Waldo Emerson: Saturn conjunct Ketu in Leo in the 12th house
- Athena Roussel: Saturn conjunct Ketu in Scorpio in the 2nd house
- Christina Onassis: Saturn conjunct Ketu in Virgo in the 5th house
- Burt Bacharach: Saturn conjunct Ketu in Scorpio in the 11th house
- Doug Flutie: Saturn conjunct Ketu in Capricorn in the 6th house

- Jennifer Gates: Saturn conjunct Ketu in Pisces in the 7th house
- Tina Turner: Saturn conjunct Ketu in Aries in the 10th house
- Paul Gauguin: Saturn conjunct Ketu in Pisces in the 8th house
- Tyra Banks: Saturn conjunct Ketu in Gemini in the 1st house

Tyra Bank's chart:

Tyra quickly rose to fame as one of the top models of the 1990s. Currently she has her own talk show, and is said to be the new Oprah Winfrey for the younger generation.

Her Saturn/Ketu is in Gemini in the 1st house. The first house represents the persona of the individual and I believe this is what gives her a unique beauty. Ketu in the 1st will make someone appear mysterious with an unusual appearance. Saturn as ruler of the 8th and 9th houses makes her magnetic and spiritual. The ruler of the 9th house in the 1st makes one spiritual and the rulership of the 8th indicates her search for meaning. As Saturn rules the 9th house it will give luck and fortune. Ketu gives it an unusual interesting quality.

The sign dispositor of Saturn/Ketu is Mercury, which gives her gifts in communications and learning. Saturn in Mercury's sign gives focus and an ability to concentrate and learn. Mercury is in the 6th house indicating her desire to help others and promote healing to the planet. Her talk show will bring awareness to the world.

The nakshatra dispositors of Saturn and Ketu are different. Ketu is in Mrigashira and Saturn is in Ardra. Ketu's nakshatra dispositor is Mars. Mars is powerfully placed in the 11th house in its own sign of Aries. This indicates great gains and connections to very powerful people.

As a model she worked with the most powerful people in her industry, working with designers Ralph Lauren, Oscar de la Renta, and Chanel. Now in the media business, she works with Oprah Winfrey and Ellen DeGeneres. She is a power to be reckoned with for future generations. Rahu is the nakshatra dispositor of Saturn. Saturn is aspected by its dispositor. This is a powerful Saturn that will give a feel of a magnetized Rahu. It is in the 7th house which can cause difficulty in marriage. So far she has not been married and is not interested. Tyra's Saturn/Ketu in the first house makes her unique and unusual. She couldn't have attained her success without it.

Interestingly, she was in the Ketu dasha from 1994-2001 when she had her rise to fame as supermodel. Ketu gave her rise and success, particularly because it magnified her powerful Saturn.

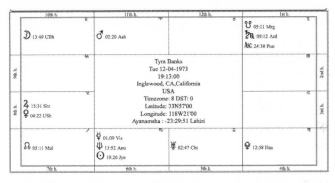

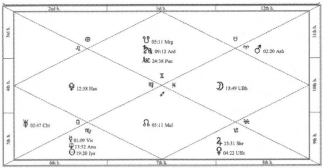

191

Conclusion

Rahu and Ketu as explored in these examples illustrate our karmic destiny. Through understanding them we will discover our own destiny and ultimately the karmas of our world.

Rahu and Ketu are the hidden aspects of a chart revealing the unknown issues that concern the deeper aspects of our soul. The soul is that which we carry from lifetime to lifetime. These hidden issues are rarely apparent, but at the time of the eclipses we can get glimpses of the secrets of our soul.

During eclipses the energy of the Earth changes energetically due to the alignment of the deeper aspects of our existence. The Sun and Moon symbolize the male and female duality of planet Earth. When the Sun, Moon and Earth align with Rahu and Ketu during eclipses the light of these luminaries is blocked out. In the darkness we come to discover our deeper issues. Even Einstein tracked the bending of light with a total solar eclipse to prove his theory of relativity.

When the light is darkened we are forced to look within and still the mind from this conscious awareness. In the dark our shadow side is revealed to provoke a healing of deep psychological and spiritual issues. These are the secrets of the soul that Rahu and Ketu will teach.

The nodes of the Moon represent the shadow side of life for they are not actually physical objects and therefore invisible. They are the points where the Moon crosses the path of the Sun around the Earth (ecliptic). Their representation concerns the forces of the psyche of the mind as in consciousness and the inner awareness of the unconscious. The conscious mind is Rahu and the unconscious mind is Ketu. Rahu concerns our desires and the materialistic world while Ketu is our unconscious mind and intuitive force that connects us to the spiritual world. But Rahu is that which gives physical comforts while Ketu takes these away, instilling suffering through loss, and a yearning to escape the suffering of this world.

The eclipses connect the deeper aspects of the duality of this world – the Sun versus Moon as seen from Earth – to the illusions of the world via Rahu and the spiritual forces of the world beyond via Ketu.

There is nothing more meaningful in this life than to discover the secrets of our existence. The pursuit of enlightenment via the study of Vedic astrology allows us to discover the purpose of our existence. This can be captured through the understanding of these points Rahu and Ketu as they align with the Sun and Moon. Through this we make sense of our world and life, and awaken to the truth of our reality. Understanding these powerful indicators can help us heal our life's issues. The willingness to see our shadows can transform our lives. This is our ultimate destiny – to free our souls from that which keeps us incarnating on the wheel of karma.

Rahu and Ketu can give us the insights to heal our relationships, which are an integral part of releasing the karmic bonds that bind us here. In addressing the hidden aspects of our personality, we discover how the ego keeps us in the realm of suffering. Once we realize that our unconscious behaviors locked in our shadows are the force that causes our own suffering, we can understand how to unlock the character flaws in our consciousness to be free from all suffering in this world. This is *moksha*, the spiritual liberation from the cycles of karma that keep us incarnating here.

The information revealed through these opposing forces of Rahu and Ketu, and the power that eclipses surface from the darkness, will unleash our karmic destiny in this life. In gratitude to these spiritual forces, may we all see the light.

Blessings from Rahu and Ketu!

~ Joni Patry

Sign Placements of Rahu and Ketu 1940-2040

Rahu	Libra	07/31/1938	02/17/1940
Ketu	Aries	07/31/1938	02/17/1940
Rahu	Virgo	02/17/1940	09/05/1941
Ketu	Pisces	02/17/1940	09/05/1941
Rahu	Leo	09/05/1941	03/25/1943
Ketu	Aquarius	09/05/1941	03/25/1943
Rahu	Cancer	03/25/1943	10/11/1944
Ketu	Capricorn	03/25/1943	10/11/1944
Rahu	Gemini	10/11/1944	05/01/1946
Ketu	Sagittarius	10/11/1944	05/01/1946
Rahu	Taurus	05/01/1946	11/18/1947
Ketu	Scorpio	05/01/1946	11/18/1947
Rahu	Aries	11/18/1947	06/06/1949
Ketu	Libra	11/18/1947	06/06/1949
Rahu	Pisces	06/06/1949	12/24/1950
Ketu	Virgo	06/06/1949	12/24/1950
Rahu	Aquarius	12/24/1950	07/12/1952
Ketu	Leo	12/24/1950	07/12/1952
Ketu	Cancer	07/12/1952	01/29/1954
Rahu	Capricorn	07/12/1952	01/29/1954

Rahu	Sagittarius	01/29/1954	08/18/1955
Ketu	Gemini	01/29/1954	08/18/1955
Rahu	Scorpio	08/18/1955	03/06/1957
Ketu	Taurus	08/18/1955	03/06/1957
Rahu	Libra	03/06/1957	09/23/1958
Ketu	Aries	03/06/1957	09/23/1958
Rahu	Virgo	09/23/1958	04/12/1960
Ketu	Pisces	09/23/1958	04/12/1960
Rahu	Leo	04/12/1960	10/30/1961
Ketu	Aquarius	04/12/1960	10/30/1961
Rahu	Cancer	10/30/1961	05/19/1963
Ketu	Capricorn	10/30/1961	05/19/1963
Rahu	Gemini	05/19/1963	12/05/1964
Ketu	Sagittarius	05/19/1963	12/05/1964
Rahu	Taurus	12/05/1964	06/24/1966
Ketu	Scorpion	12/05/1964	06/24/1966
Rahu	Aries	06/24/1966	01/11/1968
Ketu	Libra	06/24/1966	01/11/1968
Rahu	Pisces	01/11/1968	07/30/1969
Ketu	Virgo	01/11/1968	07/30/1969
Rahu	Aquarius	07/30/1969	02/16/1971
Ketu	Leo	07/30/1969	02/16/1971
Rahu	Capricorn	02/16/1971	09/05/1972
Ketu	Cancer	02/16/1971	09/05/1972

| Rahu | Sagittarius | 09/05/1972 | 03/25/1974 |
| Ketu | Gemini | 09/05/1972 | 03/25/1974 |

| Rahu | Scorpio | 03/25/1974 | 10/12/1975 |
| Ketu | Taurus | 03/25/1974 | 10/12/1975 |

| Rahu | Libra | 10/12/1975 | 04/30/1977 |
| Ketu | Aries | 10/12/1975 | 04/30/1977 |

| Rahu | Virgo | 04/30/1977 | 11/17/1978 |
| Ketu | Pisces | 04/30/1977 | 11/17/1978 |

| Rahu | Leo | 11/17/1978 | 06/05/1980 |
| Ketu | Aquarius | 11/17/1978 | 06/05/1980 |

| Rahu | Cancer | 06/05/1980 | 12/23/1981 |
| Ketu | Capricorn | 06/05/1980 | 12/23/1981 |

| Rahu | Gemini | 12/23/1981 | 07/13/1983 |
| Ketu | Sagittarius | 12/23/1981 | 07/13/1983 |

| Rahu | Taurus | 07/13/1983 | 01/29/1985 |
| Ketu | Scorpio | 07/13/1983 | 01/29/1985 |

| Rahu | Aries | 01/29/1985 | 08/18/1986 |
| Ketu | Libra | 01/29/1985 | 08/18/1986 |

| Rahu | Pisces | 08/18/1986 | 03/06/1988 |
| Ketu | Virgo | 08/18/1986 | 03/06/1988 |

| Rahu | Aquarius | 03/06/1988 | 09/23/1989 |
| Ketu | Leo | 03/06/1988 | 09/23/1989 |

| Rahu | Capricorn | 09/23/1989 | 04/12/1991 |
| Ketu | Cancer | 09/23/1989 | 04/12/1991 |

| Rahu | Sagittarius | 04/12/1991 | 10/29/1992 |
| Ketu | Gemini | 04/12/1991 | 10/29/1992 |

| Rahu | Scorpio | 10/29/1992 | 05/18/1994 |
| Ketu | Taurus | 10/29/1992 | 05/18/1994 |

| Rahu | Libra | 05/18/1994 | 12/05/1995 |
| Ketu | Aries | 05/18/1994 | 12/05/1995 |

| Rahu | Virgo | 12/05/1995 | 06/24/1997 |
| Ketu | Pisces | 12/05/1995 | 06/24/1997 |

| Rahu | Leo | 06/24/1997 | 01/11/1999 |
| Ketu | Aquarius | 06/24/1997 | 01/11/1999 |

| Rahu | Cancer | 01/11/1999 | 07/30/2000 |
| Ketu | Capricorn | 01/11/1999 | 07/30/2000 |

| Rahu | Gemini | 07/30/2000 | 02/16/2002 |
| Ketu | Sagittarius | 07/30/2000 | 02/16/2002 |

| Rahu | Taurus | 02/16/2002 | 09/05/2003 |
| Ketu | Scorpio | 02/16/2002 | 09/05/2003 |

| Rahu | Aries | 09/05/2003 | 03/24/2005 |
| Ketu | Libra | 09/05/2003 | 03/24/2005 |

| Rahu | Pisces | 03/24/2005 | 10/11/2006 |
| Ketu | Virgo | 03/24/2005 | 10/11/2006 |

| Rahu | Aquarius | 10/11/2006 | 04/29/2008 |
| Ketu | Leo | 10/11/2006 | 04/29/2008 |

| Rahu | Capricorn | 04/29/2008 | 11/16/2009 |
| Ketu | Cancer | 04/29/2008 | 11/16/2009 |

Rahu	Sagittarius	11/16/2009	06/06/2011
Ketu	Gemini	11/16/2009	06/06/2011
Rahu	Scorpion	06/06/2011	12/23/2012
Ketu	Taurus	06/06/2011	12/23/2012
Rahu	Libra	12/23/2012	07/12/2014
Ketu	Aries	12/23/2012	07/12/2014
Rahu	Virgo	07/12/2014	01/29/2016
Ketu	Pisces	07/12/2014	01/29/2016
Rahu	Leo	01/29/2016	08/17/2017
Ketu	Aquarius	01/29/2016	08/17/2017
Rahu	Cancer	08/17/2017	03/06/2019
Ketu	Capricorn	08/17/2017	03/06/2019
Rahu	Gemini	03/06/2019	09/22/2020
Ketu	Sagittarius	03/06/2019	09/22/2020
Rahu	Taurus	09/22/2020	04/12/2022
Ketu	Scorpio	09/22/2020	04/12/2022
Rahu	Aries	04/12/2022	10/30/2023
Ketu	Libra	04/12/2022	10/30/2023
Rahu	Pisces	10/30/2023	05/18/2025
Ketu	Virgo	10/30/2023	05/18/2025
Rahu	Aquarius	05/18/2025	12/05/2026
Ketu	Leo	05/18/2025	12/05/2026
Rahu	Capricorn	12/05/2026	06/23/2028
Ketu	Cancer	12/05/2026	06/23/2028

Rahu	Sagittarius	06/23/2028	01/10/2030
Ketu	Gemini	06/23/2028	01/10/2030
Rahu	Scorpio	01/10/2030	07/30/2031
Ketu	Taurus	01/10/2030	07/30/2031
Rahu	Libra	07/30/2031	02/15/2033
Ketu	Aries	07/30/2031	02/15/2033
Rahu	Virgo	02/15/2033	09/05/2034
Ketu	Pisces	02/15/2033	09/05/2034
Rahu	Leo	09/05/2034	03/24/2036
Ketu	Aquarius	09/05/2034	03/24/2036
Rahu	Cancer	03/24/2036	10/11/2037
Ketu	Capricorn	03/24/2036	10/11/2037
Rahu	Gemini	10/11/2037	04/30/2039
Ketu	Sagittarius	10/11/2037	04/30/2039
Rahu	Scorpio	04/30/2039	11/16/2040
Ketu	Taurus	04/30/2039	11/16/2040

Notes

All historical references in this book come from Wikipedia.

Chart data comes from Astrotheme: https://www.astrotheme.com/

Concepts concerning Rahu and Ketu from: *Rahu and Ketu in Predictive Astrology* by Manik Chand Jain

Chart Calculation software Parashara"s Light

Calculation used: Sidereal, Lahiri, Whole signs

Fixed Star chart: Jennifer Williams

Table for Rahu and Ketu: from BarbaraPijan http://www.barbarapijan.com/bpa/Graha/Rahu/1Rahu-MainPage.htm

Joni Patry

Joni Patry from Dallas, Texas is one of the most recognized teachers and Vedic astrologers in the world. She was a faculty member for ACVA, CVA and Instructor for online certification programs, published many books, journals and appeared on national and international television shows.

As the keynote speaker for international conferences, she has a Japanese website, and teaches in Turkey and India.

She has been awarded the 2015 Jyotish Star of the year and Dr B. V. Raman's Janma Shatamanothsava Award Jyotisha Choodamani.

She publishes an online astrological magazine, Astrologic Magazine http://astrologicmagazine.com/

In 2016 she opened the University of Vedic Astrology to provide certification for Vedic astrologers http://universityofvedicastrology.com

Joni Patry, Vedic Astrologer

Galactic Center (214) 352-2488

Website: www.galacticcenter.org

Email: joni@galacticcenter.org

Wikipedia page:
https://en.wikipedia.org/wiki/Joni-Patry

Youtube channel: Joni Patry

Facebook: Joni Patry Vedic Astrologer

Twitter @jonipatry

On-line magazine: www.astrologicmagazine.com

Become a certified Vedic astrologer via the University of Vedic Astrology: www.universityofvedicastrology.com

Made in the USA
Middletown, DE
06 March 2021